TRANSIT COOPERATIVE RESEARCH PROGRAM

TCRP RESEARCH REPORT 250

AIRPORT COOPERATIVE RESEARCH PROGRAM

ACRP RESEARCH REPORT 275

NATIONAL COOPERATIVE HIGHWAY RESEARCH PROGRAM

NCHRP RESEARCH REPORT 1129

Intermodal Passenger Facility Planning and Decision-Making for Seamless Travel

William L. Schwartz
NELSON\NYGAARD CONSULTING ASSOCIATES, INC.
Boston, MA

T0295688

IN ASSOCIATION WITH

Nico Larco and Amanda Howell
UNIVERSITY OF OREGON
Portland, OR

Louis Alcorn, Aaron Organ, and Sallye Perrin
WSP AMERICAS
New York, NY

Bree Mobley and Joe Iacobucci
SAM SCHWARTZ ENGINEERING
New York, NY

Subscriber Categories
Passenger Transportation • Planning and Forecasting • Terminals and Facilities

Research sponsored by the Federal Transit Administration in cooperation with the American Public Transportation Association, by the Federal Aviation Administration, and by the American Association of State Highway and Transportation Officials in cooperation with the Federal Highway Administration

 *Sciences Engineering Medicine*

2024

TRANSIT COOPERATIVE RESEARCH PROGRAM

The nation's growth and the need to meet mobility, environmental, and energy objectives place demands on public transit systems. Current systems, some of which are old and in need of upgrading, must expand service area, increase service frequency, and improve efficiency to serve these demands. Research is necessary to solve operating problems, adapt appropriate new technologies from other industries, and introduce innovations into the transit industry. The Transit Cooperative Research Program (TCRP) serves as one of the principal means by which the transit industry can develop innovative near-term solutions to meet demands placed on it.

The need for TCRP was originally identified in *TRB Special Report 213—Research for Public Transit: New Directions,* published in 1987 and based on a study sponsored by the Urban Mass Transportation Administration—now the Federal Transit Administration (FTA). A report by the American Public Transportation Association (APTA), *Transportation 2000,* also recognized the need for local, problem-solving research. TCRP, modeled after the successful National Cooperative Highway Research Program (NCHRP), undertakes research and other technical activities in response to the needs of transit service providers. The scope of TCRP includes various transit research fields including planning, service configuration, equipment, facilities, operations, human resources, maintenance, policy, and administrative practices.

TCRP was established under FTA sponsorship in July 1992. Proposed by the U.S. Department of Transportation, TCRP was authorized as part of the Intermodal Surface Transportation Efficiency Act of 1991 (ISTEA). On May 13, 1992, a memorandum agreement outlining TCRP operating procedures was executed by the three cooperating organizations: FTA; the National Academies of Sciences, Engineering, and Medicine, acting through the Transportation Research Board (TRB); and APTA. APTA is responsible for forming the independent governing board, designated as the TCRP Oversight and Project Selection (TOPS) Commission.

Research problem statements for TCRP are solicited periodically but may be submitted to TRB by anyone at any time. It is the responsibility of the TOPS Commission to formulate the research program by identifying the highest priority projects. As part of the evaluation, the TOPS Commission defines funding levels and expected products.

Once selected, each project is assigned to an expert panel appointed by TRB. The panels prepare project statements (requests for proposals), select contractors, and provide technical guidance and counsel throughout the life of the project. The process for developing research problem statements and selecting research agencies has been used by TRB in managing cooperative research programs since 1962. As in other TRB activities, TCRP project panels serve voluntarily without compensation.

Because research cannot have the desired effect if products fail to reach the intended audience, special emphasis is placed on disseminating TCRP results to the intended users of the research: transit agencies, service providers, and suppliers. TRB provides a series of research reports, syntheses of transit practice, and other supporting material developed by TCRP research. APTA will arrange for workshops, training aids, field visits, and other activities to ensure that results are implemented by urban and rural transit industry practitioners.

TCRP provides a forum where transit agencies can cooperatively address common operational problems. TCRP results support and complement other ongoing transit research and training programs.

TCRP RESEARCH REPORT 250

Project D-21
ISSN 2572-3782
ISBN 978-0-309-72614-6
Library of Congress Control Number 2024946281

© 2024 by the National Academy of Sciences. National Academies of Sciences, Engineering, and Medicine and the graphical logo are trademarks of the National Academy of Sciences. All rights reserved.

Published research reports of the

TRANSIT COOPERATIVE RESEARCH PROGRAM

are available from

National Academies Press
500 Fifth Street, NW, Keck 360
Washington, DC 20001

(800) 624-6242

and can be ordered through the Internet by going to
https://nap.nationalacademies.org

Printed in the United States of America

AIRPORT COOPERATIVE RESEARCH PROGRAM

Airports are vital national resources. They serve a key role in transportation of people and goods and in regional, national, and international commerce. They are where the nation's aviation system connects with other modes of transportation and where federal responsibility for managing and regulating air traffic operations intersects with the role of state and local governments that own and operate most airports. Research is necessary to solve common operating problems, to adapt appropriate new technologies from other industries, and to introduce innovations into the airport industry. The Airport Cooperative Research Program (ACRP) serves as one of the principal means by which the airport industry can develop innovative near-term solutions to meet demands placed on it.

The need for ACRP was identified in *TRB Special Report 272: Airport Research Needs: Cooperative Solutions* in 2003, based on a study sponsored by the Federal Aviation Administration (FAA). ACRP carries out applied research on problems that are shared by airport operating agencies and not being adequately addressed by existing federal research programs. ACRP is modeled after the successful National Cooperative Highway Research Program (NCHRP) and Transit Cooperative Research Program (TCRP). ACRP undertakes research and other technical activities in various airport subject areas, including design, construction, legal, maintenance, operations, safety, policy, planning, human resources, and administration. ACRP provides a forum where airport operators can cooperatively address common operational problems.

ACRP was authorized in December 2003 as part of the Vision 100—Century of Aviation Reauthorization Act. The primary participants in the ACRP are (1) an independent governing board, the ACRP Oversight Committee (AOC), appointed by the Secretary of the U.S. Department of Transportation with representation from airport operating agencies, other stakeholders, and relevant industry organizations such as the Airports Council International-North America (ACI-NA), the American Association of Airport Executives (AAAE), the National Association of State Aviation Officials (NASAO), Airlines for America (A4A), and the Airport Consultants Council (ACC) as vital links to the airport community; (2) TRB as program manager and secretariat for the governing board; and (3) the FAA as program sponsor. In October 2005, the FAA executed a contract with the National Academy of Sciences formally initiating the program.

ACRP benefits from the cooperation and participation of airport professionals, air carriers, shippers, state and local government officials, equipment and service suppliers, other airport users, and research organizations. Each of these participants has different interests and responsibilities, and each is an integral part of this cooperative research effort.

Research problem statements for ACRP are solicited periodically but may be submitted to TRB by anyone at any time. It is the responsibility of the AOC to formulate the research program by identifying the highest priority projects and defining funding levels and expected products.

Once selected, each ACRP project is assigned to an expert panel appointed by TRB. Panels include experienced practitioners and research specialists; heavy emphasis is placed on including airport professionals, the intended users of the research products. The panels prepare project statements (requests for proposals), select contractors, and provide technical guidance and counsel throughout the life of the project. The process for developing research problem statements and selecting research agencies has been used by TRB in managing cooperative research programs since 1962. As in other TRB activities, ACRP project panels serve voluntarily without compensation.

Primary emphasis is placed on disseminating ACRP results to the intended users of the research: airport operating agencies, service providers, and academic institutions. ACRP produces a series of research reports for use by airport operators, local agencies, the FAA, and other interested parties; industry associations may arrange for workshops, training aids, field visits, webinars, and other activities to ensure that results are implemented by airport industry practitioners.

ACRP RESEARCH REPORT 275

Project 03-64
ISSN 2572-3731 (Print)
ISSN 2572-374X (Online)
ISBN 978-0-309-72614-6
Library of Congress Control Number 2024946281

© 2024 by the National Academy of Sciences. National Academies of Sciences, Engineering, and Medicine and the graphical logo are trademarks of the National Academy of Sciences. All rights reserved.

Published research reports of the

AIRPORT COOPERATIVE RESEARCH PROGRAM

are available from

National Academies Press
500 Fifth Street, NW, Keck 360
Washington, DC 20001

(800) 624-6242

and can be ordered through the Internet by going to
https://nap.nationalacademies.org

Printed in the United States of America

NATIONAL COOPERATIVE HIGHWAY RESEARCH PROGRAM

Systematic, well-designed, and implementable research is the most effective way to solve many problems facing state departments of transportation (DOTs) administrators and engineers. Often, highway problems are of local or regional interest and can best be studied by state DOTs individually or in cooperation with their state universities and others. However, the accelerating growth of highway transportation results in increasingly complex problems of wide interest to highway authorities. These problems are best studied through a coordinated program of cooperative research.

Recognizing this need, the leadership of the American Association of State Highway and Transportation Officials (AASHTO) in 1962 initiated an objective national highway research program using modern scientific techniques—the National Cooperative Highway Research Program (NCHRP). NCHRP is supported on a continuing basis by funds from participating member states of AASHTO and receives the full cooperation and support of the Federal Highway Administration (FHWA), United States Department of Transportation, under Agreement No. 693JJ31950003.

The Transportation Research Board (TRB) of the National Academies of Sciences, Engineering, and Medicine was requested by AASHTO to administer the research program because of TRB's recognized objectivity and understanding of modern research practices. TRB is uniquely suited for this purpose for many reasons: TRB maintains an extensive committee structure from which authorities on any highway transportation subject may be drawn; TRB possesses avenues of communications and cooperation with federal, state, and local governmental agencies, universities, and industry; TRB's relationship to the National Academies is an insurance of objectivity; and TRB maintains a full-time staff of specialists in highway transportation matters to bring the findings of research directly to those in a position to use them.

The program is developed on the basis of research needs identified by chief administrators and other staff of the highway and transportation departments, by committees of AASHTO, and by the FHWA. Topics of the highest merit are selected by the AASHTO Special Committee on Research and Innovation (R&I), and each year R&I's recommendations are proposed to the AASHTO Board of Directors and the National Academies. Research projects to address these topics are defined by NCHRP, and qualified research agencies are selected from submitted proposals. Administration and surveillance of research contracts are the responsibilities of the National Academies and TRB.

The needs for highway research are many, and NCHRP can make significant contributions to solving highway transportation problems of mutual concern to many responsible groups. The program, however, is intended to complement, rather than to substitute for or duplicate, other highway research programs.

NCHRP RESEARCH REPORT 1129

Project 08-156
ISSN 2572-3766 (Print)
ISSN 2572-3774 (Online)
ISBN 978-0-309-72614-6
Library of Congress Control Number 2024946281

© 2024 by the National Academy of Sciences. National Academies of Sciences, Engineering, and Medicine and the graphical logo are trademarks of the National Academy of Sciences. All rights reserved.

Published research reports of the

NATIONAL COOPERATIVE HIGHWAY RESEARCH PROGRAM

are available from

National Academies Press
500 Fifth Street, NW, Keck 360
Washington, DC 20001

(800) 624-6242

and can be ordered through the Internet by going to
https://nap.nationalacademies.org

Printed in the United States of America

FOREWORD

By Dianne S. Schwager
Staff Officer
Transportation Research Board

This report describes the state of the practice, emerging lessons, and recommended practices for how intermodal passenger facilities can meet the needs of diverse users in the 21st century. The report emphasizes seamless travel and considers how customers experience intermodal passenger facilities, particularly during complex trips in an era of rapid change and the emergence of advanced technologies. This report will be used as a planning and decision-making resource for intermodal facility planners and owners, transportation providers, concerned stakeholders, and their communities.

An intermodal passenger facility is a transportation hub served by at least two modes of travel with at least one travel mode by air, rail, bus, or passenger vessel. This report:

- Presents a typology of facilities (train stations, bus stations, transit centers, and ferry/cruise ship terminals/docks) and emphasizes the intermodal components of traveling to/from and within commercial airports.
- Provides a 10-category planning framework suitable for various community contexts and governance structures and applies the planning framework to managing pickups and drop-offs as an example.
- Explains project delivery methods, funding and financing options, and data management and data stewardship strategies, including harnessing new data.
- Provides examples from existing intermodal passenger facilities, and integrated descriptions of published references provide context and additional information on specific topics.

The appendices offer additional resources and case studies addressing (A) advanced air mobility, (B) private data sources, (C) project delivery, (D) federal funding, and (E) a Denver Union Station case study.

The research was conducted by Nelson\Nygaard Consulting Associates, Inc., and a team of consultants, including the University of Oregon, Sam Schwartz Engineering, RAW International, and WSP Americas. The objective of this research was to develop a guide and decision-making framework for stakeholders to plan, implement, and operate intermodal passenger facilities that address the near- and longer-term needs in different types of communities.

The report discusses how changes in travel and other societal trends may alter future intermodal passenger facility uses. These changes include increased telework, ongoing disruptions to intercity bus service, increased adoption of digital technologies, expansion of electric vehicles for personal use and for transit, the broadening housing crisis, an aging population, and increased frequency of extreme weather events.

AUTHOR ACKNOWLEDGMENTS

The research reported herein was performed under TCRP Project D-21 by Nelson\Nygaard Consulting Associates, Inc., contractor for this study.

Bill Schwartz, AICP, Principal of Nelson\Nygaard, was Principal Investigator. Contributors to the report include Nico Larco, AIA, Professor of Architecture at the University of Oregon and Director of the Urbanism Next Center; Amanda Howell, Urbanism Next Researcher at the Sustainable Cities Institute (SCI) of the University of Oregon, now with the Oregon Department of Transportation; Sallye Perrin, Senior Vice President and National Director of P3s at WSP; Aaron Organ, Senior Consultant, Aerial Innovation at WSP; Louis Alcorn, AICP, Senior Technical Principal and Lead Consultant of Transit and Rail Finance at WSP; Bree Mobley, Senior Transportation Engineer at Sam Schwartz Engineering; and Joe Iacobucci, Senior Principal at Sam Schwartz Engineering.

Additional contributors to the research project include Alan Danaher, P.E., PTOE, AICP, PTP, Senior Vice President at WSP; Paul Wheeler, Vice President, Aerial Innovation Services at WSP; Catherine Prince, MBA, PMP, LEED AP, STP, Vice President, Climate Resilience and Sustainability at WSP; Christian Zimmer, Senior Consultant at WSP; Tim Thornton, Principal Financial Consultant at HDR (formerly at WSP); Sabrina Ortiz, Architectural Designer at Overland Partners and Researcher at Urbanism Next; Karina Macias, Senior Associate at Nelson\Nygaard and now Program Manager at Psomas; Amy Pettine, Senior Principal at Nelson\Nygaard; Sam Huffman, Associate at Nelson\Nygaard; Sophia Constantine, Associate at Nelson\Nygaard; and Mary Cay Walp, Senior Designer at Nelson\Nygaard.

CONTENTS

Intermodal Passenger Facility Planning and Decision-Making for Seamless Travel

Introduction

TCRP Research Report 250/ACRP Research Report 275/NCHRP Research Report 1129: Intermodal Passenger Facility Planning and Decision-Making for Seamless Travel is a guide for intermodal passenger facility planning and decision-making in an era of accelerated change and uncertainty. An intermodal passenger facility is a transportation hub served by at least two modes of travel with at least one travel mode being air, rail, bus, or passenger vessel. These facilities are also known as multimodal centers or terminals, airports, transit centers or stations, ferry or cruise ship terminals/docks, or mobility hubs. Intermodal passenger facilities have varying levels of activity; facilities located in more urban environments often include other commercial uses and nearby or integrated activity generators, while other facilities are exclusively for transportation.

The report discusses how changes in travel and other trends might alter future facility uses. For example, certain trends in transportation and society that began in the 2010s accelerated since 2020, including increased telework, ongoing disruptions to intercity bus service, increased adoption of digital technologies, and expansion of electric vehicles for personal use and for transit. In addition, the broadening housing crisis, an aging population, and increased frequency of extreme weather events all have implications for the future of intermodal passenger facilities.

Context for Planning and Collaborating

A typology of intermodal passenger facilities has four main components: primary transportation mode or modes at the facility, network function (how the facility connects with the broader transportation network), surrounding context (density of land use and walkability of the surrounding area), and activity generator or generators (other areas activity). (See Summary Figure 1.) At commercial airports, the key distinctions are the intermodal components within airports (airside) and intermodal connections outside airports (landside).

Each intermodal passenger facility is unique, and decisions should reflect the context and goals for that facility. Based on interviews with facility planners and owners, modal operators, and industry experts, planning falls into 10 categories. Summary Table 1 lists these 10 categories and highlights steps and decision-making considerations by category. See Chapter 4 for guidance on applying these categories.

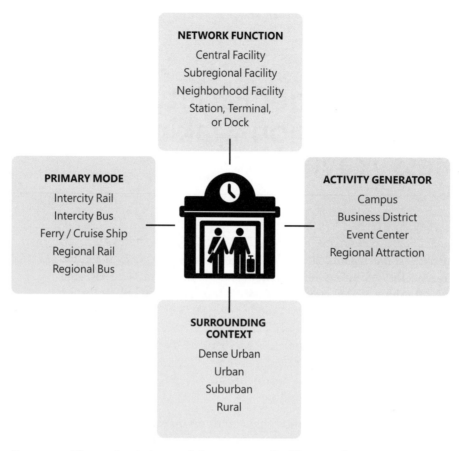

Summary Figure 1.   Intermodal passenger facility typology.

Summary Table 1.   Intermodal passenger facility planning and decision-making categories.

Planning Category		
Governance and Partnerships	Site Planning and Design	Safety and Security
Funding and Finance	Equity and Inclusion	User Experience
Permitting and Regulations	Operations and Maintenance	Data and Information Needs
	Technology and Systems	

Key Planning and Decision-Making Considerations

Future Flexibility

Intermodal passenger facility projects take many years to implement, which is a long-standing challenge that may need further investigation to identify methods of shortening the timeline. Because today's plans may not reflect tomorrow's needs, this report emphasizes the importance of planning and making decisions with flexibility and adaptability in mind. Flexibility includes designing spaces that can be reconfigured or repurposed. Adaptability includes understanding usage patterns and redeploying resources, retraining staff, or establishing new partnerships to respond to change.

Supporting Seamless Travel and the Complete Trip

The U.S. Department of Transportation (U.S. DOT) describes seamless travel in the context of the complete trip, which is the idea that any individual traveler must be able to execute every part of their trip from origin to destination regardless of location, income, or disability. Prioritizing the customer's experience means considering how different customers experience intermodal passenger facilities, particularly during complex trips. The complete trip includes seven segments. Summary Table 2 illustrates how intermodal passenger facility planners, owners, and modal providers can support each segment.

Considering Emerging Technologies

The report anticipates how new technologies such as automated vehicles and advanced air mobility (AAM) will affect intermodal travel, facility design, and space allocation. Fully

Summary Table 2.   How an intermodal passenger facility supports the complete trip.

Complete Trip Segment	Role of the Intermodal Facility
Trip planning	• Provides information on websites and other places welcoming customers and explaining how to travel to/from the facility and how to navigate it
Outdoor navigation	• Orients customers and others arriving at or leaving the facility by explaining travel options, navigation within the facility, and orientation to surrounding community
Boarding/using vehicles	• Offers clear directions to available parking, pickup and drop-off zones, or other ground transportation services • Prioritizes pedestrian safety and navigation • Ensures adequate staffing available during surge periods
Vehicle/mode transfers/payments	• Sizes passenger boarding and alighting zones adequately, particularly for passengers with luggage • Incorporates all modes, including intercity bus • Ensures that all customers have access to amenities and different fare payment options • Considers the needs of passengers with disabilities and those with limited English proficiency
Indoor/outdoor transition	• Ensures that horizontal circulation, vertical circulation, entrances, and exits are properly sized with clear wayfinding
Indoor navigation and use	• Provides attractive, comfortable, and well-illuminated spaces with inviting customer amenities
Connecting to/completing trip segments	• Facilitates safe, smooth intermodal transfers minimizing travel distances, offering needed assistance, and providing clear wayfinding

automated vehicles may someday be more common and have a transformative impact on use and management of the loading zones, surrounding streets, and parking facilities at intermodal passenger facilities. AAM, which broadly refers to emerging aviation markets and use cases for on-demand aviation in urban, suburban, and rural communities, will use both existing and new infrastructure, including airports, heliports, and vertiports (Cohen et al. 2024). Facility planners may wish to consider whether to accommodate AAM, or at least to design their facilities to not preclude AAM in the future.

Using Data and Information

Intermodal passenger facility owners and providers rely on data to understand daily operations and trends and flag issues requiring attention. The quality of available data and the use of data to make decisions varies, in part due to the lack of established practices around data management and limited understanding of how to leverage insights gleaned from data. Data-driven decision-making can enable those managing and operating inter-modal passenger facilities to better adapt to change.

As data availability and analytics capabilities continue to grow, facility planners and owners need data collection and management plans, data stewardship plans, and data-sharing agreements. For example, geolocation technology has made it easier to track people and vehicles. Transit data provided through the General Transit Feed Specification (GTFS) is now readily available, and private companies aggregate and resell data and offer analytics for monitoring travel patterns and curb usage, for example. Facility owners may need staff trained in data science to take advantage of these data sources and tools.

Selecting a Governance Model and Project Delivery Method

"Governance is the act or process of governing or overseeing the control and direction of something (such as a country or an organization)" (Merriam-Webster, n.d.). For inter-modal passenger facilities, governance typically involves multiple entities supported by strong partnerships. Effective governance and partnership agreements incorporate flexibility throughout the facility's life cycle and reflect the local stakeholder environment. Ineffective governance can contribute to project delays, cost overruns, legal disputes, and other negative impacts. Identifying the right governance model at project inception is an essential first step in project planning and sets the stage for positive outcomes. Regardless of the model chosen, successful governance of intermodal passenger facilities is built on a shared vision, identification of partners and stakeholders, and clearly defined stakeholder relationships, with the understanding that roles often change over the course of a facility's life cycle.

Once a governance model is in place and project planning and permitting are complete (scoping, environmental evaluation and clearance, property acquisition, initial business case, and financial plan), the next step is to select a method of project delivery. Appendix C provides more details on available project delivery methods, including structures and timelines.

Funding and Financing Intermodal Passenger Facility Projects

Because intermodal passenger facility projects are often costly and complex undertakings requiring substantial financial resources, owners typically work with multiple entities to explore many sources of funding, financing options, and partnerships to complete and maintain facility projects. The process of choosing among funding programs and financing approaches includes:

- Conducting the initial project assessment,
- Establishing the base financial condition,
- Identifying funding and financing requirements, and
- Preparing grant applications.

The report explains these steps, provides detailed information on funding programs and financing mechanisms, and provides use case of the Denver Union Station redevelopment project.

Conclusion

Each intermodal passenger facility is unique. The planning and decision-making process should reflect its uniqueness as well as its relationship to the local context, its surrounding environment, and the broader community. At the same time, the intermodal passenger facility's main function is to serve people undertaking a journey. By prioritizing the experience of the customer, regardless of income, ability, or spoken language, planners, owners, and providers can better adapt to changing trends and make informed decisions. Efforts to advance the complete trip concept, expand mobility as a service (MaaS) to include all modes of transportation, emphasize effective governance, broaden partnerships, and better manage facility pickup and drop-off can all lead to improved facility operations and an enhanced user experience. The following are additional key takeaways from the research effort.

Collaborate Early and Often

Intermodal passenger facility planners, owners, and modal providers need to regularly collaborate with each other and with external stakeholders. This is an ongoing need that begins with governance and continues with partnerships. Owners, providers, and other partners should always be considering the customer's travel experience traveling to, within, and from the entire facility, not just using one mode of travel. Collaboration also includes forming and maintaining strong partnerships with external stakeholders to address non-transportation matters that can affect a facility, such as coordinating responses to extreme weather events or working to address the housing crisis.

Identify Ways to Streamline Intermodal Passenger Facility Projects

Intermodal passenger facility projects take many years to implement. As projects advance, construction costs continue to escalate; in addition, changes to the climate are accelerating, and plans developed today may be obsolete on project completion. More research may be needed on streamlining intermodal passenger facility projects to ensure that they address current needs and are affordable.

Plan with Flexibility in Mind and Adapt Accordingly

Even with shorter implementation time frames, intermodal travel will continue to evolve, and emerging technologies will continue to change travel behavior. Planning with flexibility and adaptability means assuming decisions made today will need to be revised in the future. This means working to avoid being constrained by decisions that will be hard to reverse.

Collect Data More Often and Share It More Broadly

Facility owners and modal providers need to regularly collect data that measure usage patterns and then use these data to improve facility operations and the user experience. This means regularly conducting passenger surveys, measuring how people enter and exit a facility, investing in automated systems to collect data, and sharing the data, including through open sources and in ways that are agnostic to the individual mode or the technology used.

CHAPTER 1

Introduction

TCRP Research Report 250/ACRP Research Report 275/NCHRP Research Report 1129: Inter-modal Passenger Facility Planning and Decision-Making for Seamless Travel is a guide for intermodal passenger facility planning and decision-making in an era of accelerated change and uncertainty. It combines research and analysis, practitioner interviews, and discussions of published reports. Its intended audience is those who plan, own, and manage intermodal passenger facilities, as well as the transportation providers that serve these facilities. It is a resource for others who consult on or interact with intermodal passenger facilities, such as government agencies, real estate developers, and the broader community.

Intermodal passenger facility projects addressed in this report include new facilities, expansions, and renovations. Since each project is guided by a facility owner's specific needs and priorities, the report provides context and knowledge of important trends to support future decisions.

The report emphasizes two key themes applicable to all intermodal passenger facilities:

- The intermodal passenger facility can play an increasingly important role in supporting seamless travel by prioritizing the customer experience in planning, decision-making, and daily operations.
- In an era of changing conditions for travel, demographics, the environment, and technology, flexibility and adaptability are increasingly important.

What Is an Intermodal Passenger Facility?

An intermodal passenger facility is a transportation hub served by at least two modes of travel with at least one travel mode being air, rail, bus, or passenger vessel. These facilities are also known as multimodal centers or terminals, airports, transit centers or stations, ferry or cruise ship terminals/docks, or mobility hubs. (Some practitioners refer to intermodal passenger facilities as mobility hubs, and while all intermodal passenger facilities are mobility hubs, not all mobility hubs are intermodal passenger facilities. For example, a mobility hub served by one local bus route or a hub with no transit service is not, for the purposes of this research, an intermodal passenger facility. These types of hubs are often known as neighborhood hubs, micromobility hubs, or local hubs.) For the purposes of this report, a further distinction is made for airports, which have publicly accessible landside components and secure airside components. Intermodal passenger facilities have varying levels of activity; facilities located in more urban environments often include other commercial uses and nearby or integrated activity generators, while other facilities are exclusively for transportation.

Prioritizing the Customer Experience for Seamless Travel

The U.S. Department of Transportation (U.S. DOT) describes seamless travel in the context of the complete trip, the idea that any individual traveler must be able to execute every part of their trip from origin to destination regardless of location, income, or disability. Prioritizing the customer's experience means considering how different customers experience intermodal passenger facilities, particularly during complex trips. This includes trips that may require purchasing multiple tickets; transporting, checking, and claiming baggage; passing through security screening or customs and immigration; and navigating unfamiliar spaces. For travelers with disabilities, those who speak a different language, or those with low incomes, completing complex trips can be even more stressful or impractical.

Throughout this report, reference is made to four categories of intermodal passenger facility user groups:

- **Customers:** transportation passengers and other visitors who use or interact with intermodal passenger facilities.
- **Planners:** professionals who plan intermodal passenger facility projects or plan new facilities.
- **Owners:** public or private entities that own, manage, or operate intermodal passenger facilities, as well as their employees (owner-employees).
- **Providers:** airlines, ferry and cruise ship operators, public transportation agencies, and other shared-mode transportation providers.

An intermodal passenger facility has a larger ecosystem of stakeholders, and this is discussed further in Chapter 7.

Planners, owners, and providers all play a role in facilitating seamless travel, which typically begins and ends beyond the sphere of the intermodal passenger facility and includes entering, using, transferring, and exiting the facility. The research uses a typology framework to place intermodal passenger facilities within the community context, which can help broaden the reach of facilities and strengthen neighborhood partnerships. In addition, the research takes into consideration other facility users [e.g., visitors, service-provider employees (e.g., bus operators), tenants, and vendors].

Flexibility and Adaptability in an Uncertain Future

Designing, constructing, and maintaining intermodal passenger facilities is a complex undertaking. Rapid cost escalations and implementation delays are common. A project can take 10 years or longer to construct, often following a multiyear planning and permitting process. Assumptions made during the planning phase may no longer apply. Decisions made today cannot fully anticipate the future as intermodal transportation continues to evolve and changes occur in the private sector, government policy, and society at large.

This report discusses how changes in travel and other trends might alter how people will use intermodal passenger facilities in the future and offers ways to plan accordingly. It suggests resources to support decision-making and provides examples of how other facility planners and owners have invested in features and amenities to serve their customers. It emphasizes the importance of flexibility and adaptability. Flexibility includes designing or programming spaces that can be reconfigured or repurposed. Adaptability includes understanding usage patterns and redeploying resources, retraining staff, or establishing new partnerships if warranted.

To measure changes in usage and other patterns, this report describes ways to obtain, collect, and analyze data and measure performance. It also describes different models of project governance and project delivery and emphasizes the importance of establishing and maintaining strong partnerships. The report also offers information on project funding and financing.

How to Navigate the Report

Following this introduction, the report is organized into eight additional chapters, a reference section, a list of abbreviations, and five appendices. See Exhibit 1 for a summary of main body of the report.

Hyperlinks, Callouts, and Icons

This report includes internal hyperlinks, text boxes, and icons that are placed in the margin. Internal hyperlinks enable online readers to navigate to internal report topics. External hyperlinks enable online readers to easily locate relevant reports and other resources. Text boxes highlight information compiled during the research effort, including stakeholder interviews, workshop comments, and other important information.

Hyperlinks

This report makes extensive use of embedded hyperlinks. These direct online readers to related sections of the report and to external sources and materials.

Text Boxes

This report uses grey-shaded text boxes to highlight events, research findings, intermodal passenger facility projects, and notable practices.

Exhibit 1. Summary of report.

Chapter 2 **History of Intermodal Passenger Facilities Through 2020**	This chapter offers a timeline of intermodal passenger facilities and intercity transportation from the early 1900s through 2020, noting key policy and legislative milestones, transformative external events, and changes in technology, business, environment, and society affecting how people travel.
Chapter 3 **Recent Trends and Implications**	This chapter describes trends in and implications for intermodal passenger facilities since 2020, organizing the discussion into two broad categories: (1) transportation and (2) society, business, the environment, and technology. Companion Appendix A is a primer on advanced air mobility (AAM), which is a recent trend with implications for intermodal passenger facilities.
Chapter 4 **A Typology of Intermodal Passenger Facilities**	This chapter categorizes intermodal passenger facilities by primary transportation mode or modes, network function, surrounding context, and activity generator or generators. For airports with scheduled commercial service, it discusses the intermodal components within airports (airside) and outside airports (landside).
Chapter 5 **Planning and Decision-Making Framework**	This chapter introduces a framework for planning and decision-making, using a user-centric approach and considering current trends, and it applies the framework to managing passenger pickups and drop-offs, a critical but often challenging component of intermodal passenger facilities.
Chapter 6 **Data and Information Needs**	This chapter explains how to plan and manage data collection, including methods, approaches to data stewardship, and the use of data-sharing agreements. It describes new sources of data and discusses data used for different travel modes and provides examples of using technology and systems to measure facility performance. Companion Appendix B provides information on private data sources.
Chapter 7 **Governance and Partnerships**	This chapter explains the essential elements of intermodal passenger facility governance, and the assignment of roles and responsibilities throughout the facility's life cycle. It introduces different models of project delivery and offers an overview of private development partnerships with references to resources and examples of joint development. Companion Appendix C offers a detailed discussion of project delivery methods.
Chapter 8 **Funding and Financing**	This chapter explains ways to choose the right funding program and financing approach and summarizes the funding, financing, and innovative delivery options available. Companion Appendix D provides tables with funding sources available as of this report's publication. Companion Appendix E presents a case study of Denver Union Station's innovative financing and project delivery approach.
Chapter 9 **Conclusion**	This chapter provides a brief summary of key takeaways from the report.

Published Reports, Checklists, and Decision Points

Potentially useful reports feature this icon placed in the report margin.

Useful checklists feature this icon placed in the report margin.

Narratives describing potential decisions feature this icon placed in the report margin.

Typology and Planning Framework

The typology chapter (Chapter 4) categorizes intermodal transportation facilities by primary transportation mode or modes, network function, surrounding context, and activity generator or generators. It presents examples of existing intermodal passenger facilities, including facilities discussed in stakeholder interviews. It also includes examples of using typologies and goals in the facility planning process.

The planning and decision-making framework chapter (Chapter 5) introduces 10 categories of planning and decision-making and includes selected steps and decision-making considerations for each planning category as examples. Following a discussion of the complete trip in support of seamless travel, it presents an example of applying the typology and planning categories for managing pickups and drop-offs. This example may be applied to decision-making processes.

Existing Intermodal Passenger Facility Guidance

Almost all intermodal passenger facility projects are complex multiyear efforts, and no single report or guide can possibly cover all project elements. Guidance and manuals are available from multiple sources, including:

- At the federal level, the FTA, FAA, FRA, and FHWA oversee programs, issue regulations, and provide direction on modal projects.
- National organizations such as AASHTO and the National Association of City Transportation Officials (NACTO), as well as architecture, engineering, and construction industry associations, publish widely used standards and guidance resources.
- TRB's Cooperative Research Program has also published many relevant syntheses, web resources, and reports. The research team reviewed CRP reports and other resources and has identified the most useful publications for practitioners. Notable resources include an icon in the margin. The first such resource is *TCRP Research Report 165: Transit Capacity and Quality of Service Manual* (TCQSM; Kittelson & Associates, Inc., et al. 2013).

Transit Capacity and Quality of Service Manual, Third Edition

TCRP Research Report 165: Transit Capacity and Quality of Service Manual, Third Edition (Kittelson & Associates, Inc., et al. 2013) is a cornerstone of the TCRP report series. It has consistently been TCRP's most downloaded and viewed document and is used throughout the United States by public transportation practitioners and other industry professionals. The TCQSM covers the principles and practices of transit capacity for all transit modes and quality of service from the customer's viewpoint.

The Third Edition of the TCQSM, published in 2013, includes background, statistics, and graphics on the types of public transportation, and a framework for measuring transit availability, comfort, and convenience. The manual documents quantitative techniques for calculating the capacity and other operational characteristics of bus, rail, demand-responsive, and ferry transit services, as well as for transit stops, stations, and terminals. It describes station facilities of all sizes, ranging from individual bus stops to large intermodal passenger facilities, and includes concepts and detailed methodologies applicable to different operating environments and complexities.

TCQSM Third Edition, Chapter 9 (Ferry Service and Ferry Facilities)

Chapter 9 of the TCQSM provides information on terminals for water transportation, covering intermodal integrations such as transfers to park-and-ride lots; feeder bus services; roll-on, roll-off bus services (for auto ferries); and nearby rail connections. It distinguishes between passenger-only ferries such as in the New York and San Francisco Bay regions and passenger/vehicle ferries such as in metropolitan Seattle.

TCQSM Third Edition, Chapter 10: Station Capacity

Chapter 10 of the TCQSM includes extensive information on horizontal and vertical circulation within intermodal passenger facilities and includes ways to analyze levels of service. The horizontal circulation section explains the capacity and sizing of walkways, moving walkways, waiting platforms, and multi-activity passenger circulation areas such as the concourse at Grand Central Terminal in New York City. The vertical circulation section addresses the capacity and sizing of stairways, escalators, and elevators and the relationship between street level, concourses, and platform movements. This chapter also describes the circulation and queueing space requirements for fare collection machines and fare gates.

TCQSM Fourth Edition

The Fourth Edition of the TCQSM is being prepared. This edition will address recent developments in the public transportation industry, including a greater concern for equity. It will offer analytical procedures for assessing intermodal facility capacity and level of service, including increased use of simulation modeling. This includes simulating motor vehicle and bus movements to size pickup/drop-off zones, waiting areas, and parking areas. Such simulations help planners evaluate different vehicle staging and parking configurations.

The Fourth Edition will assess the impacts of electrification of ferry vessels on terminal space requirements, as well as the capacity impacts of alternate docking configurations to size gangways and vehicle holding areas.

Airport Terminal Design Information

ACRP Report 25: Airport Passenger Terminal Planning and Design, Volume 1: Guidebook (Landrum & Brown et al. 2010) provides information for planning and developing airport passenger terminals and to assist users in analyzing common issues related to airport terminal planning and design. It explores the passenger terminal planning process and provides, in a single reference document, the important criteria and requirements needed to help address emerging trends and develop potential solutions for airport passenger terminals. Volume 1 addresses the airside, terminal building, and landside components of the terminal complex.

Station Siting Resources

Guidance on siting intercity rail stations and high-capacity transit stations is available from the National Cooperative Rail Research Program (NCRRP), FRA, and TCRP.

Passenger Rail Stations

NCRRP Research Report 6: Guidebook for Intercity Passenger Rail Service and Development (Morgan et al. 2016) includes a chapter on design and construction that cites the following factors to consider when evaluating intercity passenger rail stations:

- Provision of facilities/services for connecting modes not available at site.
- Revisions to existing connecting services required.
- Proximity to major facilities and destinations.
- Effect on current railroad operations at existing station.
- Potential funding sources and costs.
- Development/redevelopment and tax base enhancement potential.
- Neighborhood impacts.
- Metropolitan urban form and socioeconomic impacts (Morgan et al. 2016).

FRA's Railroad Corridor Transportation Plans: A Guidance Manual emphasizes the importance of intermodal transportation, stating, "Every effort should be made to have each station serve as a regional intermodal passenger terminal for all forms of regional and local transportation systems" (Federal Railroad Administration 2005). The report also suggests having at least one station located in or near a city's central business district and, in larger regions, the report suggests siting suburban stations near a major highway (Federal Railroad Administration 2005).

High-Capacity Transit Stations

TCRP Research Report 153: Guidelines for Providing Access to Public Transportation Stations addresses planning and design for access to high-capacity transit stations, including guidelines for arranging and integrating various station design elements, and includes an eight-step planning process for effective station access planning (Coffel et al. 2012).

Mobility Hub Guidance

Numerous resources are available on mobility hubs including from the Institute of Transportation Engineers (ITE; ITE, n.d.) and the Shared Use Mobility Center (SUMC; SUMC, n.d.), and others such as the Broward County Metropolitan Planning Organization (MPO; Broward MPO 2021), and the San Diego Association of Governments (SANDAG; SANDAG, n.d.). Given the range of applications—from intercity rail stations to neighborhood bus stops—the decision process for siting mobility hubs is context specific.

CHAPTER 2

History of Intermodal Passenger Facilities Through 2020

Introduction

This chapter provides a brief history of the evolution of intermodal passenger facilities, beginning with the first train stations and urban rail systems, describing how intercity travel evolved following the expansion of the Interstate highway system and the growth of commercial aviation. It considers how external events, national policy, and changes in technology, consumer behavior, and business have influenced intermodal passenger facilities, setting the stage for a closer examination of recent trends and implications in the next chapter.

The history and evolution fall into five eras of differing durations (see Figure 1).

- **Pre-1970:** Rise and decline of intercity travel by train and bus.
- **1970–1989:** A changing business climate for rail, bus, and air travel.
- **1990–2009:** Technology transforms business and consumer behavior.
- **2010–2019:** New mobility era.
- **2020 and beyond:** Remote/hybrid work, climate adaptation, and automation (see Chapter 3).

Pre-1970: Rise and Decline of Intercity Travel by Train and Bus

The U.S. transportation system underwent dramatic changes between the 1900s and 1960s, transforming the movement of both people and goods. Most of the country's iconic train stations were constructed in this period (1900s–1930s), and many that survived are historic stations with new development. Private investors constructed urban rail transit services (streetcars, underground subways, and elevated lines) during this period. Numerous new transit stations included transfer points to other transit services, and some included station or area amenities that spurred higher-density development, a precursor to today's transit-oriented development (TOD) districts. In the 1950s, the federal government began building the Interstate highway system, and passenger airport construction/expansion took place throughout the United States.

The intercity bus system, which began as hundreds of independent companies in the early 1900s, consolidated into a few major companies, including Greyhound, which by the beginning of World War II, had 4,750 stations and employed about 10,000 people (Cook 2019). By the late 1950s, highway expansion and increasingly affordable air travel contributed to a decline in intercity bus and rail travel.

The federal government established several separately funded modal organizations to regulate modes of travel, including the agencies now known as FHWA, FAA, and FTA. Separated funding for each agency limited intermodal planning (Horowitz and Thompson 1994). By the 1960s, most U.S. cities were characterized by an auto-oriented built environment, the passenger railroad industry was in decline, and transit experienced major ridership declines.

PRE-1970: RISE AND DECLINE OF INTERCITY TRAVEL BY TRAIN AND BUS

1890s–1930s Large-scale railroad terminal construction serving more passengers and more functions

1927 First park-and-ride lot and first bus-rail transfer facility opens in Philadelphia

1946 Baby boom and suburban migration begins

Late 1955 Travel by air surpasses travel by rail

1956 National Interstate and Defense Highways Act

1969 First automated vehicle location (AVL) system introduced in Chicago

1913 New Grand Central Terminal opens in New York

1914–1918 World War I

1939–1945 World War II

1946 U.S. transit ridership at all-time high

Late 1950s Greyhound has nearly 5,000 stations and 10,000 employees

1960s Air and car travel grows; rail, bus, and transit travel declines

1970–1989: A CHANGING BUSINESS CLIMATE FOR RAIL, BUS, AND AIR TRAVEL

1971 National Railroad Passenger Corporation (Amtrak) established

1978 Airline Deregulation Act

1970s Energy crisis and gas shortages

1982 Airport Improvement Program

1970 Airport and Airway Development Act

1975 Amtrak introduces intercity bus ticketing

1980s Urban rail transit investments for new systems and stations

1983 Greyhound drivers' strike

1990-2009: TECHNOLOGY TRANSFORMS BUSINESS AND CONSUMER BEHAVIOR

1990 Urban rail system expansion continues

1991 Use of highway funds for transit permitted

1991 Intermodal Surface Transportation Efficiency Act (ISTEA)

Late 1990s First "Chinatown" buses between New York and Boston

2001 9/11 terrorist attacks

2006 Google transit offers real-time transit data in Portland, Oregon

2007 First iPhone

1990 Americans with Disabilities Act

Early 1990 Air travel grows significantly

1995 Amtrak launches first website

Early 2000s Growth of mobile computing

2005 Milwaukee airport/Amtrak access project completed

2006 Hurricane Katrina

2007 60% of Greyhound's market share in northeast U.S. taken by "Chinatown" buses.

2010-2019: NEW MOBILITY ERA

2012 Superstorm Sandy exposes NY subway system vulnerabilities

2012 Transit app introduced

2017 U.K.-based First Group acquires Greyhound and its real estate holdings

2012 Ridehailing services via transportation network companies (TNCs) begin

2014 Nashville Airport regulates TNCs; many airports soon follow

2018 Waymo begins testing autonomous taxi service in Phoenix, AZ

2020 AND BEYOND: REMOTE/HYBRID WORK, CLIMATE ADAPTATION, AND AUTOMATION

2020 Global pandemic leads to dramatic increase in hybrid and remote work

2021 Infrastructure Investment and Jobs Act (IIJA)

2022 Advanced Air Mobility Coordination and Leadership Act

2023 Deployment of autonomous robotaxis in San Francisco generates ongoing controversy. Cruise ceases operations while Waymo continues operating.

2020s Significant growth in battery electric vehicle sales

2021 First Group sells Greyhound bus operations to FlixBus; continues to sell bus stations for redevelopment

2022 Inflation Reduction Act

Federal Legislation / Policy

External Events

Figure 1.   Timeline of U.S. intercity travel and intermodal passenger facilities.

1970–1989: A Changing Business Climate for Rail, Bus, and Air Travel

The Rail Passenger Service Act of 1970 created the National Railroad Passenger Corporation, later known as Amtrak, to assume control of intercity rail following bankruptcies of private passenger railroad companies. Following a period of decline, including neglect and abandonment of some historic train stations, the 1980s saw the rehabilitation of legacy rail stations and the restoration/expansion of commuter rail services.

In 1975, Amtrak initiated a program to encourage intermodal travel by providing travelers with information on bus interchange routes. Auto dependence continued to grow, with vehicle ownership rates steadily rising between 1970 and 1990 (Rodrigue 2024). The intercity bus industry continued to see ridership declines, and Greyhound Lines experienced major driver strikes in 1983 and 1990. Further bus industry consolidations, bankruptcy filings, and ownership changes took place. In transit, new or expanded rapid transit networks developed in many U.S. cities, some with stations featuring TOD, including agency-led joint development projects.

In aviation, a spate of airline hijackings led to increased passenger screening requirements. This helped lead to the premature closure of the former TWA terminal at Kansas City's Mid-Continent International Airport (MCI). When the terminal opened in 1972, its design was driven by TWA's requirement for a "drive to your gate" concept, with flight gates only 75 feet from the roadway. The cost of installing security checkpoints at each gate area rather than at a centralized area was prohibitive. As a result, passenger services (restrooms, retail, etc.) were nonexistent downstream of the security checkpoint in the gate area (Airports Worldwide, n.d.).

The 1978 Airline Deregulation Act was transformative in helping to open up air travel to many more people. Established airlines rushed to gain or preserve access to the most lucrative routes. New airlines quickly formed. Fierce competition resulted, which drove fares down. Passengers flocked to airports in record numbers (National Air and Space Museum 2021).

1990–2009: Technology Transforms Business and Consumer Behavior

The passage of the Intermodal Surface Transportation Efficiency Act of 1991 (ISTEA) paved the way for a new era of intermodal passenger transportation planning. Previously, federal transportation policy and funding generally focused on individual modes rather than intermodal transportation (U.S. Government Accountability Office 2007). ISTEA allowed the use of federal highway program funds for other highway or transit projects, among other changes.

By the early 1990s, Amtrak-operated trains began carrying more commuter passengers than intercity passengers, and transit ridership was slowly starting to increase following a period of decline (Bureau of Transportation Statistics 2013). This era also witnessed significant growth in air travel in the United States (Statista Research Department 2024). This led to efforts to improve intermodal connections to airports, and the first Amtrak station with direct access to an airport opened in Milwaukee in 2005. The earliest bikesharing and carsharing systems were launched in the late 1990s (Shaheen et al. 2020b), and carsharing firm Zipcar was established in 2000.

In the early 2000s, several bus companies began offering curbside service between New York, Boston, Philadelphia, and Washington, DC, at far lower fares than bus-terminal–based operators, affecting Greyhound's market share in the northeast.

Major technological change also defined this period, including the growth of the Internet. Amtrak launched its website in 1995, and although online booking would not be available for a few years, the website provided schedule information (Amtrak, n.d.). Home broadband use

> **Transformative Events**
>
> Events that helped to transform the management and operation of intermodal passenger facilities included the terrorist attacks of September 11, 2001, and major storms such as Hurricane Katrina (2005). The Department of Homeland Security and the Transportation Security Administration were both created in the wake of 9/11. New airport security measures limited gate access to employees and ticketed passengers, requiring customers to arrive earlier. With customers spending more time in terminals, airport operators added space for restaurants, bars, lounges, and shopping.
>
> In 2005, Hurricane Katrina made landfall in New Orleans, becoming one of the worst natural disasters in the history of the United States and highlighting the vulnerability of critical infrastructure to massive weather events (U.S. Government Accountability Office 2006).

expanded rapidly, from about 1% to 62% in just 10 years (Pew Research Center 2024). This changed how travelers could access information, albeit on each provider's website.

The first Internet-enabled phones were available in the early 2000s, but the release of the first iPhone in 2007 and other touchscreen-enabled devices soon thereafter transformed how millions of travelers could communicate and access information. Application (app) developers introduced smartphone apps, including many for travel purposes.

2010–2019: New Mobility Era

Broad access to smartphone apps led to the development of app-enabled on-demand mobility options, which have continued to transform behavior.

Transportation Network Companies

A transportation network company (TNC) is a for-hire vehicle (FHV) ridehailing service with one paid driver and at least one paying passenger. In 2012, TNCs such as Uber and Lyft started offering on-demand (not pre-arranged) ridehailing in the United States. By 2014, the demand for TNC services had grown enough that Nashville International Airport was the first airport to have an agreement with TNC providers (Leiner and Adler 2020). By 2016, TNCs were permitted to operate at 60 airports, and by 2019, Lyft had agreements with 368 airports in North America (Leiner and Adler 2020). As TNCs proliferated, many airports and cities experienced increased congestion and competition for curb space, with some establishing dedicated zones for where these activities could take place. City transportation departments responded by establishing operating rules and pickup zones. Intermodal passenger facility planners and owners and their agency partners learned lessons from the rapid growth of ridehailing, including the value of flexibility and adaptability; these lessons apply to future intermodal passenger facility planning.

Bikesharing and Scooter Sharing Programs

Bikesharing provides users with on-demand access to bicycles at a variety of pickup and drop-off locations for one-way (point-to-point) or roundtrip travel. E-scooters, short for electric scooters, are light, battery-powered vehicles ridden while standing up. E-scooter sharing arrived in Santa Monica in 2017 and expanded across the United States quickly thereafter (Fonseca 2019). In 2010, bikesharing and e-scooter sharing saw 321,000 total trips, growing to 136 million trips by 2019, with 86 million (63%) trips via scooter (NACTO 2020). Station-based bikesharing trips were limited to a few cities, such as San Francisco, Boston, Chicago, Honolulu, New York City, and Washington, DC.

This era also saw a number of U.S. cities investing in improved bicycling and walking infrastructure and implementing Vision Zero plans to eliminate traffic-related fatalities and severe injuries. These investments and initiatives have enabled more people to access intermodal passenger facilities by walking and bicycling.

Availability of Real-Time Transit Data

In the transit industry, dissemination of real-time data became far more widespread through the use of automatic vehicle location (AVL) equipment (APTA 2021). This enabled agencies to provide real-time vehicle arrival displays in stations and at stops and to disseminate information to app developers. The plethora of smartphone apps with real-time data pushed directly to travelers permitted personal trip planning without consulting information screens or asking for assistance.

Growth and Potential of Battery Electric Buses for Transit

In 2018, when *TCRP Synthesis 130: Battery Electric Buses—State of the Practice* was published, there were at least 13 battery electric bus (BEB) models available and more than 70 U.S. transit agencies with BEB deployments, with 600 BEBs on order or in service. The report describes the growth and potential of the BEB market and challenges many transit agencies face while deploying BEB technology (Hanlin et al. 2018).

Electric Vehicle Sales Growth

Sales of battery electric vehicles (EVs) in the United States have grown rapidly, from approximately 10,000 in 2011 to more than 240,000 in 2019 (U.S. Department of Energy, n.d.; Argonne National Laboratory, n.d.). As of 2020, nearly 1.8 million EVs were registered in the United States, three times as many as were registered in 2016 (Desilver 2021).

Focus on Improving the Airport Passenger Experience

ACRP Research Report 157: Improving the Airport Customer Experience describes notable and emerging practices in airport customer service management to increase customer satisfaction (Boudreau et al. 2016). Terminal renovation projects began at several airports, including a major renovation of New York's LaGuardia Airport Terminals A and B. As airport terminals expanded, navigating terminals required longer walks within them, increasing the need for airlines to assist passengers who were unable or not confident in their ability to travel to and from airline gates. *ACRP Research Report 177: Enhancing Airports for Aging Travelers and Persons with Disabilities* provides information on pedestrian wayfinding for older adults and people with disabilities to help them independently navigate airports [Harding et al. 2017; also see the Airport Terminal Planning Advisory Circular published in 2018 (Federal Aviation Administration 2018)].

Automated Vehicle Investments and Testing

Automated vehicles (AVs) are vehicles that automate certain driving systems that do not require human input. SAE International has defined six levels of autonomy for vehicles, from

Level 0, with no automation, to Level 5, where the steering wheel becomes optional for the vehicle (InterVISTAS Consulting, Inc., forthcoming). The new mobility era saw growth in automation, with features and elements being integrated into personal vehicles. Private companies began testing automated vehicles on closed tracks and subsequently on city streets. In 2017, some automakers were predicting that fully automated vehicles would be available by 2020 (Madrigal 2017).

Important Changes Outside of Passenger Transportation

Other important trends that accelerated during the 2010s and continue to have implications for intermodal passenger facilities include the growth of e-commerce, rapid increases in housing costs and expanded housing shortages, and increased frequency of extreme weather events. According to a United Nations (UN) report, from 2000 to 2019, there were 7,348 major natural disasters. By comparison, 1980 through 1999 had 4,212 natural disasters (UN Office for Disaster Risk Reduction 2020).

CHAPTER 3

Recent Trends and Implications

This chapter describes trends and implications for intermodal passenger facilities from 2020 onward. It organizes the discussion into two broad categories: (1) transportation and (2) society, business, the environment, and technology.

2020 and Beyond: Remote/Hybrid Work, Climate Adaptation, and Automation

The 2020s represent a decade of continuous advances with implications for intermodal passenger facilities. Certain trends that began in the 2010s (the new mobility era) continued, but have been affected by advances in technology, changes in the private sector, climate change, and other factors.

Trends in Transportation

Growth in Telework

In August 2020, eight months after the Centers for Disease Control issued its first announcement about what became the COVID-19 pandemic, 36% of people in the United States reported living in a household where at least one person substituted telework for in-person work (Bureau of Transportation Statistics, n.d.). Some workers who began teleworking during the pandemic became remote employees, and others returned to the office on a limited basis with hybrid work arrangements.

In 2023, 12.7% of full-time employees worked from home, and 28.2% of all employees had adapted to a hybrid work model (Haan 2023). In certain U.S. cities, the share of people commuting to central business districts continues to be far lower than during pre-pandemic levels. While the number of commute trips fell, other home-based trips increased, leading to an overall increase in the number of trips nationally. At the publishing of this report, a pattern may be emerging where hybrid-eligible employees work remotely on Mondays and Fridays (WSJ Podcasts 2023).

Implications

While the future of work remains uncertain, the idea that the pandemic fundamentally reshaped work—and, by extension, commute patterns—is prevalent (Parker et al. 2022). Many transit agencies have experienced ridership declines, particularly on commuter-oriented routes, and face revenue shortfalls. This has implications for commuter-oriented intermodal passenger facilities, many of which have seen a rise in retail vacancies. While peak travel may not return to pre-pandemic levels for many years, usage patterns are likely to shift throughout the day as transit operators adapt to different demand patterns. As of this report's publication, this remained an area of active change and development, with an eventual steady state still uncertain.

If retail becomes a less viable use for intermodal passenger facilities, this could have implications for customers using the facilities for travel. If customers miss their connection or if a trip is canceled, passenger waiting areas that do not have amenities can diminish the user experience.

Intercity Bus Industry Disruptions

The intercity bus industry continues to evolve. United Kingdom–based First Group, which had owned Greyhound and many of its bus terminals since 2007, sold bus operations to Munich, Germany–based FlixBus and retained control of its remaining U.S. real estate holdings. First Group sold bus stations in several cities in 2020 and 2021, and in 2022, sold its remaining holdings to a private equity firm, which has since been closing additional bus stations.

Implications

The loss of more bus stations is an issue of equity and transportation access. Many intercity bus passengers have lower incomes. All passengers need safe and secure places to wait for buses and to access restrooms, food concessions, and other amenities typically found in passenger terminals. Integration of intercity bus with other modes, even beyond Amtrak and state services, will remain important but could be difficult to achieve. Partnerships and funding will be critical elements.

The Chaddick Institute at DePaul University publishes an annual outlook for the intercity bus industry. The 2023 outlook predicted continued loss of safe and comfortable places for passengers to wait for a bus, noting:

- Bus service has been relocated from bus stations to intermodal passenger facilities, train stations, convenience stores, transit hubs, curbside spots, and some airports.
- The loss of passenger facility amenities creates issues for passengers transferring late at night or early in the morning, with lengthy layovers, or during inclement weather, creating a burden on disadvantaged groups who depend heavily on bus travel.
- Bus services have been relocated to less desirable locations, sometimes outside of city centers.
- While federal regulations require funding recipients to provide "reasonable access" to intercity bus lines at public transit facilities, the fees for this access are not set in the regulations, and some of the fees being charged lead intercity bus operators to find a less costly location (Schwieterman et al. 2023).

A December 2023 *Wall Street Journal* article noted that the loss of traditional bus stations "highlights a plight confronting millions of travelers, many on lower incomes, that attracts far less attention than passenger rail or aviation" (Harrison 2023). The article notes, "as more centrally located bus stations close, it is not clear what will take their place. Bus operators are looking for public-sector funding to finance new facilities while some municipal officials say it is on the [bus companies] to provide safe and reliable places for riders to wait" (Harrison 2023).

Chaddick's 2024 outlook offered the following predictions:

- Passenger traffic, now at 85%–90% of the pre-pandemic level, will fully recover by 2026—a change from Chadwick's 2023 outlook. Driver shortages and other problems could slow the recovery, which will be uneven across regions, but the trends are favorable.
- The serious problems stemming from the closing of traditional bus stations will worsen before they get better. The accumulating effects of the closings will hurt disadvantaged populations and further hamper the image of some bus lines and bus travel generally.

- Public policies will gradually swing in the industry's favor as the growing hardships facing disabled and lower-income travelers on long-distance trips and the success of state-supported bus systems reduce the indifference toward bus travel among many public agencies. Federal resources and new tools showcasing the importance of the U.S. intercity bus network will augment this trend.
- Improvements to the FlixBus/Greyhound, Megabus, and Trailways booking platforms will help attract new traffic. More itinerary options, reserved seating, bus-tracker tools, and other conveniences are giving consumers better choices. Still, finding the best schedule option remains far more cumbersome than for air or rail travel.
- Increases in fares will outpace inflation in the next several years, improving profit margins. Rising load factors and the strong demand for travel holiday season (for 2023) indicate that carriers will have more pricing power than in the past.
- Cooperation between Amtrak (and its state supporters) and intercity bus lines enters a new and more exciting phase as carriers and policymakers harness the benefits of further integrating these modes. Such integration will be enhanced by the Infrastructure Investment and Jobs Act [also known as the Bipartisan Infrastructure Law (BIL)], which will encourage states and local governments to plan for better bus and train services in tandem (Schwieterman et al. 2023).

Zero-Emission Buses and Transit Fleet Electrification

According to *TCRP Research Report 219: Guidebook for Deploying Zero-Emission Transit Buses*, the zero-emission bus (ZEB) market, including BEBs and fuel-cell electric buses, has begun to see growth (Linscott and Posner 2021). As of 2021, U.S. transit agencies had seen more than 1,300 ZEBs delivered or awarded, although this remains a small share of the U.S. transit bus fleet (Horadam and Posner 2022). State-level initiatives will contribute to further growth. For example, a 2020 law established requirements for New Jersey Transit to move toward 100% ZEB purchases by 2032 (New Jersey Transit, n.d.). New Jersey Transit uses motor coaches for commuter services, including trips to the Port Authority Bus Terminal in New York, for which a major terminal renovation project is underway (Port Authority of New York and New Jersey, n.d.). The project includes substantial investments in electric charging facilities for BEBs. (See discussion of Port Authority Bus Terminal project in Chapter 5.) California's Zero-Emission Airport Shuttle Regulation, adopted in 2019, requires airport shuttle operators to transition to 100% zero-emission vehicle (ZEV) technologies (California Air Resources Board 2019).

As transit agencies respond to state mandates to convert fleets from diesel fuel, this will result in the purchase of additional ZEBs. While the shift to electrification has hit some headwinds related to charging infrastructure and vehicle cost and maintenance, the trend continues to be toward an increase in electric fleets.

Implications

The electrification of the U.S. transit fleet requires further implementation of charging facilities, and some intermodal passenger facilities will be part of the charging network. BEB charging infrastructure requires space and power and, at scale, power demands will be significant (Linscott and Posner 2021).

Digitalization/Mobility as a Service

Transit agencies and other mobility providers around the United States continue to explore mobility as a service (MaaS) platforms to support more fluid and linked transportation systems. [MaaS is also known as public mobility. See *TRB Special Report 139: Between Public and Private Mobility: Examining the Rise of Technology-Enabled Transportation Services* (Transportation

Research Board Committee for Review of Innovative Urban Mobility Services 2016)]. As conceived, MaaS platforms would enable travelers to plan, book, and pay for multiple transportation services in a single digital interface (Shaheen et al. 2020a). These kinds of platforms are designed to make multimodal travel seamless by shifting the burden of integrating multiple modes from the traveler to the MaaS provider (Moody and Alves 2022). Implementation of MaaS typically requires multiple agencies to coordinate unless a single provider owns multiple modes.

For example, the Southern Minnesota MaaS Platform Pilot Project is one example of a state-led multiagency trip planning platform and is illustrated in Figure 2. Led by the Minnesota Department of Transportation (MnDOT), the project is a collaboration of nearly 20 transit agencies and various technology vendors, including the Transit app, to create a regional trip planning platform that supports fixed-route transit, flexible transit, and paratransit, ridesharing, and micromobility (bicycles, scooters, bikesharing, scooter sharing) in southern Minnesota (Shared Use Mobility Center 2023).

In Houston, Texas, the ConnectSmart application is a multiagency partnership of transit agencies, Texas DOT, FHWA, and communities aimed at reducing the use of single-occupancy vehicles, improving safety, and reducing traffic. The mobile app provides users with available and personalized intermodal travel options and costs, transportation system updates, predictive travel times, and intermodal navigation, and it includes a mobility wallet (Texas Department of Transportation 2024).

The increase in digitization includes other transportation elements such as parking, bicycling infrastructure, carsharing, and ridehailing/TNCs. At intermodal passenger facilities, this has led to conversion of spaces for other uses and the establishment of active mobility zones, such as at airports in Los Angeles and San Francisco.

Implications

While MaaS may hold promise in increasing transit travel and reducing private car use, it is still early in its development; testing of models of managing and deploying MaaS continues. To be successful, MaaS implementations must focus equally on the technical aspect of MaaS and the need for strong partnerships between municipalities, transit agencies, MaaS providers, transportation service providers, businesses, and user groups.

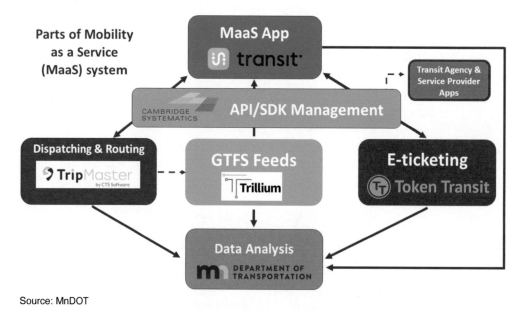

Source: MnDOT

Figure 2.   Minnesota DOT regional trip planning platform.

While its future remains uncertain, MaaS can be an important complement to intermodal passenger facilities since it supports mode connectivity for travelers. Even if not fully implemented as conceived, further integration of multimodal fare payment and intermodal transfers remains an important goal within the industry. As with other innovations, its broad adoption also raises issues of equity for certain individuals who are not fully engaged in the digital world. Having access to a smartphone, understanding how to use and navigate apps, having a data plan, and having a bank account are all barriers that will reduce or bar access for many individuals.

The increased use of digital technology will continue to transform how most customers use intermodal passenger facilities, including trip booking, navigating facilities, the check-in process, and security screening.

Shared Automated Vehicle Testing and Deployment

Shared automated vehicles (SAVs), which operate similarly to TNCs but are driverless and owned and operated by companies rather than individuals, are the subject of much discussion and debate. Perfecting the technology that enables vehicles to drive themselves under all conditions has proven difficult, so the timeline of widespread SAV deployment has repeatedly shifted in recent years (Chafkin 2022). Companies such as Waymo and Cruise began offering for-hire transportation in unattended vehicles in San Francisco and Phoenix and aimed to expand to other cities (Ohnsman 2022). The deployment of SAVs has included technical safety challenges, regulatory issues, and some erosion of public trust in companies offering SAV transportation.

While early projections of AV deployment posited them as fulfilling a wide range of use cases and transportation needs, recent deployments have pointed to a potentially more limited deployment. Much like TNCs, SAVs achieve their greatest efficiencies in denser areas where more potential riders take short trips. In less dense areas, demand is lower, requiring vehicles to travel longer distances, often without paying passengers. It is uncertain what minimum densities are necessary for SAV services, but their viability may depend on operating costs and how much riders will pay. In short, the places where these services may be most profitable are often the most congested parts of our largest cities, where transit service is more concentrated and highly competitive.

Implications

Though the future is uncertain, AVs could affect intermodal passenger facilities if and when these vehicles become widespread. Since SAVs would likely operate like TNCs, the impacts could be similar. Like ridehailing/TNCs, growth in SAVs could increase the demand for pickup/drop-off space and could increase curbside congestion as they reposition themselves after drop-offs or travel empty to pick up passengers (also known as deadheading). SAVs would also typically rely on users with smartphones who have data plans and the means to link credit or debit cards. In addition, because SAVs would operate as fleets with no driver, companies will require dedicated spaces for vehicle staging or parking and maintenance activities. It is uncertain if the growth in SAVs will then reduce car ownership or parking demand, particularly at airports, where parking is often a major source of revenue for airport operators.

Recent deployments in San Francisco have presented challenges for emergency services, including preventing AVs from entering cordoned off areas and the inability to verbally direct AVs to reposition. Such instances may present emergency management challenges at intermodal passenger facilities. Further, pedestrian safety issues prevail.

Another looming question is whether SAVs will complement or compete with transit. If the companies can lower operating costs, SAVs may meet first-/last-mile needs and extend transit's reach. Conversely, SAVs might directly compete with transit, affecting ridership by offering more direct connections. Studies of shared mobility services to date describe a mixed record (Shaheen et al. 2020a).

Advanced Air Mobility

Advanced air mobility (AAM) broadly refers to emerging aviation markets and use cases for on-demand and scheduled aviation in urban, suburban, and rural communities. The most recent FAA reauthorization defines AAM as a transportation system that is composed of urban air mobility and regional air mobility using manned or unmanned aircraft (Congress.gov 2023). AAM includes local use cases of about a 50-mile radius in rural or urban areas and intraregional use cases of up to a few hundred miles within or between urban and rural areas. AAM enables consumers to access air mobility, logistics, and emergency services by dispatching or using innovative aircraft and enabling technologies through an integrated and connected multimodal network across the ground, waterways, and skies (Cohen et al. 2024).

As envisioned, AAM will feature innovative technologies, such as vertical takeoff and landing (VTOL) aircraft powered by electric batteries or hydrogen, and it will use both existing and new infrastructure, including airports, heliports, and vertiports (Cohen et al. 2024). Use cases include air taxis, airport feeder services, goods movement, and humanitarian assistance.

Implications

Larger airports often serve as intermodal passenger facilities where rail, air, surface, and micro-transportation options often meet. AAM presents opportunities for airports of all sizes to increase transportation services. *ACRP Research Report 243: Urban Air Mobility, An Airport Perspective* offers resources and tools for evaluating AAM opportunities and challenges (Mallela et al. 2023). It assesses the market opportunities, describes different business cases, and offers strategies for AAM integration. It includes a toolkit that is designed to help airport owners assess readiness and that offers resources for advancing readiness levels.

Implications for intermodal ground passenger facilities are less developed than for airports. In general, as with SAVs, the locations where AAM business opportunities would appear to be strongest are also places where operating aircraft is likely to be more difficult. New York City is a good example, where helicopter traffic is a source of public outcry (McGeehan and Gold 2021). Examples of intermodal passenger facility development for AAM include heliport redevelopment. The City of New York in 2023 introduced its vision for updating the Downtown Manhattan Heliport located at Pier 6 on the East River to include the necessary infrastructure to accommodate electric VTOL aircraft. This vision includes intermodal integrations with electric cargo bikes for coordination of maritime, air, and micro-cargo delivery (NYC: The Official Website of the City of New York 2023).

A 2024 Planning Advisory Service (PAS) report from the American Planning Association considers the community's role in AAM. *PAS Report 606: Planning for Advanced Air Mobility* emphasizes the importance of learning about AAM and participating in conversations with state and federal officials. It describes potential impacts of noise, privacy, visual pollution, energy use and emissions, and land use compatibility, which could affect public perceptions of AAM and have an array of effects on communities and planning practices. It offers information on these potential impacts and how land use, zoning, infrastructure siting, and other planning and policy levers may serve as mitigation strategies (Cohen et al. 2024). Intermodal ground passenger facility owners and planners can also benefit from this participatory approach.

According to PAS Report 606, while AAM presents potential opportunities for localities, negative community perceptions could pose challenges to AAM adoption and mainstreaming.

The report also emphasizes the importance of social equity issues associated with AAM, such as affordability and who benefits from or bears the impacts of AAM, and the need to integrate AAM into existing multimodal transportation networks (Cohen et al. 2024). For new intermodal passenger facilities or existing facilities located in areas without current groundside transportation, network integrations will be a key consideration. (In this report, see Station Siting Resources in Chapter 1, Travel to and from Airports in Chapter 4, Managing Pickups and Drop-offs in Chapter 5.)

ACRP Research Report 243 offers ways for intermodal passenger facility owners to consider what to do about AAM. While focused on airports, a readiness checklist and an interactive toolkit help to address readiness for urban air mobility (UAM) activity and then make a go/no-go decision by categorizing readiness into the four levels of:

- No go,
- Not now,
- Slow go, and
- Go now (Mallela et al. 2023).

For those in all levels except no go, see Appendix A for a comprehensive discussion of AAM, including a summary of recent ACRP research, ongoing federal coordination activities, use cases, and implications for airports and other intermodal passenger facilities.

Other Transportation Trends

Growth in Private Micromobility Ownership

According to a presentation given by McKinsey and Company at the Micromobility World Conference in 2023, the private ownership of micromobility is expected to double, with the growth of shared models increasing seven times by 2025. E-scooters will also see sizable growth (Descant 2023). The growth in micromobility will likely require dedication of additional space for e-scooters and bicycles at certain intermodal passenger facilities.

Sharp Rise in Motor Vehicle and Pedestrian-Involved Crashes

According to *TRB's Critical Issues in Transportation for 2024 and Beyond*, annual traffic-related fatalities grew to almost 43,000 in 2021 and 2022, about 10,000 more than in 2011. Pedestrian and bicyclist fatalities and fatality rates have also increased sharply; fatalities reached 8,300, roughly 3,300 more in 2021 than in 2010 (Transportation Research Board 2024). Prioritizing pedestrian safety at intermodal passenger facilities is especially important in pickup and drop-off zones, roadway crossings, and other areas where pedestrians and vehicles interact.

Availability of New Funding for Amtrak and High-Speed Rail

The 2021 passage of the Infrastructure Investment and Jobs Act (IIJA) included $66 billion in additional rail funding to eliminate Amtrak's maintenance backlog, modernize the Northeast Corridor, and invest in high-speed rail (HSR). Funded HSR projects include the ongoing Central Valley HSR project in California and a new HSR corridor between Las Vegas and Southern California. The IIJA also funds the following HSR corridor planning projects:

- Between Oregon, Washington, and British Columbia (Cascadia HSR Corridor)
- Dallas–Fort Worth to Houston, Texas
- Charlotte, North Carolina, to Atlanta, Georgia
- Antelope Valley, California
- Atlanta–Chattanooga–Nashville–Memphis Corridor

Additional projects receiving funding include new conventional rail corridors, extensions to existing routes, and improvements to existing routes (U.S. Department of Transportation, Federal Railroad Administration 2023).

Trends in Society, Business, the Environment, and Technology

Broadening Housing Crisis

According to the 2023 Annual Homeless Assessment Report from the U.S. Department of Housing and Urban Development, "on a single night in 2023, roughly 653,100 people—or about 20 of every 10,000 people in the United States—were experiencing homelessness" (U.S. Department of Housing and Urban Development 2023). Six in 10 people were experiencing sheltered homelessness—that is, in an emergency shelter, transitional housing, or safe haven program—while the remaining four in 10 were experiencing unsheltered homelessness in places not meant for human habitation (U.S. Department of Housing and Urban Development 2023).

The housing crisis, which has been particularly acute in cities like Los Angeles and San Francisco, is continuing to grow nationwide. Metropolitan areas that had enough housing in 2012 are now experiencing shortages, and the homelessness crisis is worsening as a result (Badger and Washington 2022). Increasing rent rates are also contributing to more individuals experiencing homelessness because as there is an increased likelihood of an inability to pay rent on time. During the pandemic, many states and cities established eviction moratoriums, which prevented qualifying individuals from being evicted due to unpaid rent, but as moratoriums get lifted, people that are unable to pay rent may end up in a state of homelessness.

Intermodal passenger facility owners and providers are experiencing an increase in the number of people experiencing homelessness, with impacts on vehicles, facilities, employees, service quality, and on housed passengers. This includes individuals seeking shelter within and around facilities and on transit vehicles (Zapata et al. 2024).

Implications

Intermodal passenger facilities throughout the United States have been affected as increasing numbers of people experiencing homelessness seek out shelter, safe spaces, and hygiene facilities in transportation facilities and vehicles. This is particularly acute in cities with high housing costs. *TCRP Research Report 242: Homelessness: A Guide for Public Transportation* describes current approaches and best practices that are responsive to people who are experiencing homelessness (Zapata et al. 2024). It identifies a range of initiatives that agencies can undertake to address the effects of homelessness on public transportation services and facilities and support people experiencing homelessness. These include partnerships with other stakeholders to jointly pursue multifaceted community goals pertaining to homelessness.

The ongoing housing crisis means that owners and providers may need to invest human and capital resources to support people experiencing homelessness. *TCRP Research Report 242* dedicates a chapter to this topic, providing resources on outreach and emergency response services and activities, outlining transit agency staff roles, and identifying training in support of people experiencing homelessness.

ACRP Research Report 254: Strategies to Address Homelessness at Airports provides airports and stakeholders with resources and suggested practices to respond, in a comprehensive and humane manner, to people experiencing homelessness by working together with local communities to provide support while ensuring safety and security at the airport (Fordham et al. 2023).

Stakeholder Workshop Discussion of Unhoused Individuals

The research team conducted a workshop with representatives of transit agencies and intermodal passenger facilities. The workshop included a focused conversation on unhoused individuals, leading to the following takeaways:

- Safety, both actual and perceptual, is the most difficult aspect to navigate. Some riders may not feel safe in a station with a substantial number of individuals perceived as unhoused, and this can deter them from using the station.
- Retailers are a huge driver of image, and some stores may opt to leave a location because of high concentrations of unhoused individuals. This can make the location undesirable for other retailers. Store vacancies can diminish non-rider traffic, which can then lead to more unhoused individuals spending time in stations.

This also has staffing implications, requiring more security personnel or the creation of new positions such as restroom or track attendants. Increased staffing also means increased training, and for many of these security-related jobs, individuals require substantive training.

Extreme Weather Events and Climate Adaptation

Severe storms, damaging floods and wildfires, and other extreme weather are increasing in frequency and impact (U.S. Global Change Research Program 2018). In 2023, the United States experienced 28 weather/climate disaster events, with losses exceeding one billion dollars and with 492 direct or indirect fatalities (Smith 2024). Such events are expected to increase in frequency and impact (U.S. Global Change Research Program 2018). Figure 3 presents a timeline of inflation-adjusted U.S. billion-dollar disaster events between 1980 and 2023.

Implications

Flooding, major snow events, and other extreme weather can lead to costly shutdowns and result in damage to intermodal passenger facilities, requiring costly repairs and investments in more resilient systems that can withstand and recover from disruptions.

Chronic stressors such as extreme temperature can have a cumulative, long-term impact on the infrastructure and the people who use intermodal passenger facilities. Extreme heat events can cause discomfort and a multitude of human health issues, especially when combined with humidity. Unhoused individuals often ride transit vehicles and visit facilities with air conditioning during periods of excessive heat. For more information, see the Broadening Housing Crisis discussion earlier in this chapter.

Higher temperatures and humidity can also make it harder for mechanical equipment, like air-cooled chillers and transformers, to shed excess heat, thereby leading to accelerated degradation of equipment and premature equipment failure. Warmer temperatures also greatly increase building cooling demands and associated costs, particularly for maintenance activities.

It is important to consider the risks (both the impact and consequences) of these climate-induced stressors and other risks on intermodal passengers and adjacent communities. Planning for future climate conditions is critical to ensure an optimal level of service for the users and for system performance.

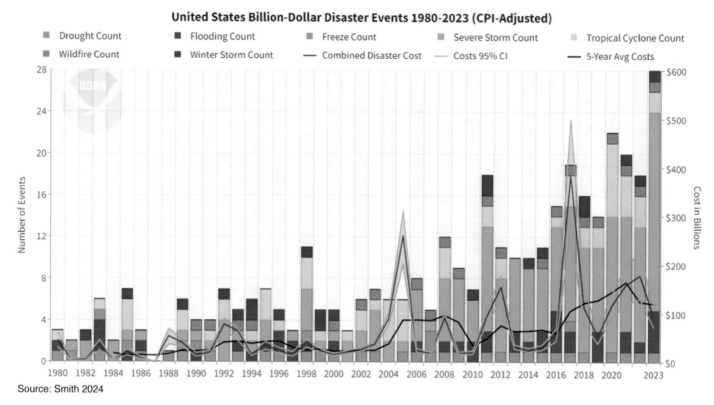

Source: Smith 2024

Figure 3.   U.S. billion-dollar disaster events 1980–2023 (CPI adjusted).

Recent intermodal facility projects have incorporated resiliency planning and risk mitigation. For example, Orlando International Airport designed its new Terminal C drainage for a 100-year storm event, and recent upgrades to the San Francisco Downtown Ferry Terminal and the Colman Dock in Seattle included major investments to withstand earthquakes.

TRB Special Report 340: Investing in Transportation Resilience: A Framework for Informed Choices (Committee on Transportation Resilience Metrics 2021) reviews current transportation agency practices for evaluating resilience and conducting investment analysis and adding resilience. It presents trend data, synthesizes current transportation system resilience practices, summarizes research and analytical methods, and proposes a decision-support framework that includes asset identification, capacity and vulnerability analysis, hazard assessments, and risk assessments. Application of the framework includes stakeholder identification and cost–benefit analyses.

ACRP Report 147: Climate Change Adaptation Planning: Risk Assessment for Airports provides a guide to help airport practitioners understand the specific impacts climate change may have on their airport, to develop adaptation actions, and to incorporate those actions into the airport's planning processes. This guide first assists practitioners in understanding their airport's climate change risks and then guides them through a variety of mitigation scenarios and examples (Dewberry et al. 2015).

Aging Population and Growth from Immigration

Based on U.S. Census Bureau population forecasts, in the next two decades, the U.S. traveling public will consist of a significantly higher proportion of older adults (65+), with nearly one in four people projected to be an older adult by 2060 (Vespa et al. 2018). Beginning in 2030, immigration is also expected to become the primary driver of population growth (Vespa et al. 2018).

Implications

As the U.S. traveling population ages, a larger share of travelers may have mobility limitations, which in turn will increase the demand for assistance in navigating public facilities. The Americans with Disabilities Act (ADA) and state and local regulations require intermodal passenger facility planners, owners, and modal providers to design and provide accessible transportation facilities and services. For more information, see *ACRP Research Report 177: Enhancing Airport Wayfinding for Aging Travelers and Persons with Disabilities* (Harding et al. 2017).

Focus on Equity and Addressing Past Harms

Increasingly, agencies and organizations around the United States are including equity in decision-making and strategic planning efforts. This includes the U.S. DOT, which added equity as a strategic goal for the first time in its 2022–2026 strategic plan (U.S. Department of Transportation 2023b). This focus includes addressing the impacts that past transportation and other major infrastructure projects have had on disadvantaged, underserved, and overburdened communities.

Acknowledging the negative effects of certain projects, such as highways that divided communities, the IIJA includes funding for the Reconnecting Communities Pilot. This initiative aims to support efforts to restore community connectivity by removing, retrofitting, mitigating, or replacing transportation infrastructure.

Implications

Integration of equity into intermodal passenger facility decision-making includes planning, design or redesign, management, and the integration of new modes. This includes working with external stakeholders to include community groups in the planning process. (See Chapter 7.) For facilities that include intercity bus transportation, considering equity means working to integrate these services within the facility or accommodating passengers in waiting areas, offering ticketing services, and granting access to other amenities.

> ### Considering Equity in San Jose and San Francisco
>
> Intermodal passenger facilities can be part of a larger equity conversation. For example, a project at Diridon Station in San Jose includes raising heavy rail tracks to stitch two neighborhoods back together at the street level. As another example, the San Francisco Bay Area Water Emergency Transportation Authority (aka San Francisco Bay Ferry) lowered its ferry fares and changed its schedule to encourage more riders and change the perception that ferries are a premium product.

Continued Growth in EV Ownership

Between 2020 and 2022, U.S. battery EV sales grew rapidly, with more than 750,000 vehicles sold in 2022. As with BEBs, EV charging infrastructure, particularly rapid charging options, have been slow to develop and will take time to reach a critical mass in certain parts of the United States.

Ongoing ACRP Research Project 03-71, "Guidance for Planning for Future Vehicle Growth at Airports," will ultimately provide information for airport operators to inventory and assess the anticipated growth in electrification needs for vehicles, aircraft, and mobile equipment.

This information will cover charging infrastructure needs, site planning, maintenance, financial considerations, resiliency, risks and hazard mitigation, and other technical, operational, and administrative concerns.

NCHRP Synthesis 605: Electric Vehicle Charging: Strategies and Programs describes strategies and practices that can help in preparation for the widespread development of EV charging facilities as the technology emerges and matures. The report explores progress and gaps in EV charging infrastructure from the perspective of state DOTs, using their experience to identify standards for future deployment of EV infrastructure (Sturgill et al. 2023).

Implications

To accomplish large-scale EV charging, facility owners will need to consider the quantity of electrical power needed, whether to purchase electricity or generate it on their own, and where to place transformers. ACRP Research Project 03-71 should provide information applicable to a broad range of intermodal passenger facilities.

EV charging for fleet vehicle and facility employees will vary by facility according to agency needs, resources, and governing policies. The demand for private passenger car EV charging is more difficult to predict. Over time, airports, future high-speed rail stations, and other intercity intermodal passenger facilities may expand access to fast chargers, perhaps in conjunction with traditional fueling stations.

Customers parking in the long term may wish to obtain a charge so they can have a fully charged vehicle on returning from travel, but such arrangements could require relocating charged vehicles to free up the charger for another vehicle. As of this report's publication, the rental car sector's EV commitments were in transition. In early 2022, Hertz announced it would sell about a third of its electric-vehicle fleet worldwide, or about 20,000 vehicles, in a reversal of its earlier strategy (Glickman 2024).

Use of Intermodal Passenger Facilities as Emergency Shelters

The use of intermodal passenger facilities as places to shelter people is not new. During the Cold War, many public buildings served as designated fallout shelters to be used in the event of a nuclear attack. As large public spaces with emergency power sources, certain facilities are capable of sheltering people in emergency circumstances. This has included warming or cooling facilities, evacuation centers during severe storms, and temporary housing for homeless individuals including, most recently, temporary housing for migrants when local shelters were full (Emanual 2024).

Implications

As the frequency of extreme weather (severe storms, excessive heat, or extreme cold) increases, intermodal passenger facilities can expect to see more use for temporary shelter. Owners and providers should consider establishing or expanding contingency plans for such circumstances and train personnel accordingly. They should establish or strengthen partnerships with government and community partners to ensure effective collaboration.

Summary of Potentially Important Trends

The trends discussed in this chapter represent a time of increased uncertainty, from changes in travel behavior to acceleration in technology. This combination makes it more difficult to make decisions, particularly for choices that are difficult to undo. In some circumstances, planning for flexibility may be appropriate. Table 1 summarizes ways in which transportation and other trends may affect intermodal passenger facility customers, owners, and providers. Chapter 6 offers additional suggestions on how to incorporate these trends into the decision-making process.

Table 1.   How current trends may affect customers, owners, and modal providers.

Topic	Customers	Owners	Providers
Telework	Reduced commuter foot traffic. Potential negative perceptions toward public transportation.	Lower retail activity. Need for more security resources.	Reduced ridership and revenues. Less predictable demand/need to alter schedules.
Intercity bus station closures	Relocation of bus boarding areas to sidewalks and other locations without amenities. Diminished user experience.	Pressure will increase to integrate intercity bus services into facilities at affordable fees.	Need for collaboration with public entities and facility owners to find ways to serve customers.
MaaS and digitization and fare payment	Improved options to plan, book, pay, and navigate. Need for fare payment alternatives for those unbanked or unable or unwilling to use digital options.	Ongoing need to integrate and update systems and technology. Management of partnerships.	More pressure to integrate with other platforms and to form new partnerships.
Shared AVs	Uncertain future and consumer adoption.	Need for agreements with municipalities and providers.	More pressure to deliver sustainable business models.
Bus fleet changes	Higher provider capital costs may lead to higher fares.	Need to invest in fleet charging infrastructure. More bus layover space requirements. Reduced ventilation requirements.	New infrastructure investments. Higher capital costs. Schedule changes to accommodate charging.
AAM	Potential improved connections to more remote locations, including access via small airports.	Plan for accommodating aircraft takeoff and landing. Integration of ground access at airports without any services.	New choices on where to invest in facilities and infrastructure.
Housing crisis	Concern about personal safety.	Need to trail staff and partner with social service agencies. Increased investments in security. Creation of segmented areas (i.e., access limited to ticketed passengers).	Need to train staff and partner with social service agencies.
Climate change and extreme weather	Increased demand for weather-protected spaces.	Infrastructure upgrades. Staff training for emergencies. Use of facilities as shelters.	Schedule disruptions. Increased contingency planning.
Aging population	Increased leisure travel as baby boom generation retires. Need for more travel support services.	Increased off-peak facility use. Demand for more travel support services.	Demand for more travel support services. Reduced revenues from more travel at reduced fares.
Equity focus	More attention paid to needs of intercity bus travelers.	Investment decisions increasingly require equity evaluations.	Fare revenue risks.
Growth in EV ownership	Demand for charging resources when parking long term.	Uncertainties around economics and coordination of commercial charging. Provision of space for non-revenue fleet charging.	Decisions about investments in fleet vehicles. Meeting government or agency board mandates.

CHAPTER 4

A Typology of Intermodal Passenger Facilities

Introduction

As explained in Chapter 1, an intermodal passenger facility is a transportation hub served by at least two modes of travel with at least one travel mode being air, rail, bus, ferry, or passenger vessel. Intermodal passenger facilities are present throughout the United States in a variety of contexts and serve local, regional, interregional, and international travelers. Some are standalone facilities, meaning they provide access to another transportation mode and may be part of a network but are distinct from other passenger facilities in that network such as Amtrak stations, Greyhound bus stations, or a city's main airport.

This chapter presents a typology of intermodal passenger facilities. The typology features four main components, as illustrated in Figure 4. For airports, the discussion covers intermodal components both within airports (airside) and outside airports (landside).

Categories of Intermodal Ground Passenger Facilities

The categories of intermodal ground transportation facilities are primary transportation mode or modes, network function, surrounding context, and activity generator or generators.

Primary Transportation Mode

The primary transportation mode represents the main mode or modes of travel the facility serves such as intercity rail, intercity bus, ferry service, cruise ship, regional rail (both commuter rail and subway), and regional bus (both commuter bus and other bus service).

Network Function

Intermodal passenger facilities with a primary function of facilitating travel by rail, bus, and ferry, and passenger vessel fall into one of four categories: central; subregional; neighborhood; or station, terminal, or dock, and range in level of complexity.

Central Facility

A central facility functions as a city's or region's main intermodal transportation hub and typically features multiple rail lines or bus routes. Many central facilities are in or near central business districts. Central facilities typically see the highest use within the overall network.

Subregional Facility

A subregional facility typically serves as a secondary transportation center that provides intermodal connections (e.g., subway and rail) and connections to the region's central facility. Subregional facilities may also offer intercity rail or bus connections.

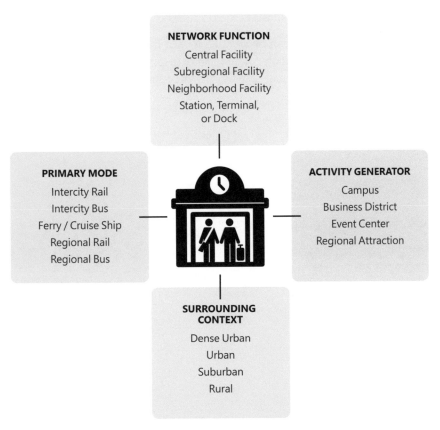

Figure 4.   Intermodal ground passenger facility typology.

Neighborhood Facility

A neighborhood facility offers limited intermodal connections and provides local area access with links to a larger regional network.

Station, Terminal, or Dock

Some rail or bus stations are in more isolated locations and include intercity rail or bus stations, regional rail stations, or connections to passenger-vessel terminals/docks. These typically feature few if any secondary transit connections.

Surrounding Context

The amount of density and the extent of nearby or integrated development are key attributes of the surrounding environment. The typology uses urban, suburban, and rural contexts and considers four categories of population density: dense urban, urban, suburban, and rural.

Dense Urban

Intermodal ground passenger facilities located in dense urban areas, such as central business districts in large cities, typically function as central facilities and offer multiple modes. These facilities often include major developments that generate considerable activity.

Urban

In most cities, intermodal ground passenger facilities in urban areas include downtown transit centers and train stations. Such facilities may include a single public transportation mode such as a regional bus service. They may function either as central or subregional facilities.

Suburban

Facilities in suburban contexts can be situated within town centers or adjacent to regional roadway systems. Within the suburban context, parking supply can be a distinguishing characteristic. Functions include subregional, neighborhood, or station, terminal, or dock.

Rural

The rural context applies to individual facilities in areas with low density. These can be bus or rail stations or ferry docks.

> **Considering Pedestrian Circulation**
>
> Intermodal ground passenger facilities in lower-density areas may not support walking or bicycling. However, even when such facilities are auto-oriented, internal pedestrian circulation elements are vital and should be safe and fully accessible.

Activity Generator

The activity generator describes area development integrated with or adjacent to other intermodal ground passenger facilities. These developments can include medical and educational campuses, business districts, event centers, and major attractions. Business districts anchoring passenger facilities can range from traditional downtowns to office parks, and walking environments can vary accordingly. Event centers such as sports arenas have unique peaking characteristics, and major attractions may see seasonal variations in demand.

Intermodal Ground Passenger Facility Examples

Table 2 provides examples of intermodal ground passenger facilities that the research team interviewed representatives from, applies the typology categories, and shows the modes of transportation served. The table includes central, subregional, and neighborhood facilities in different contexts in terms of density and activity generated by surrounding developments.

Intermodal Components of Airports

The FAA categorizes U.S. airports according to their share of annual U.S. commercial enplanements, and as of 2022, the United States had 31 large-hub airports and 33 medium-hub airports that served at least 0.25% of total enplanements (Federal Aviation Administration 2023). Passenger travel at airports includes ground access (travel to and from airport), known as landside, and travel within terminals, known as airside. This report focuses on large-hub and medium-hub airports.

Travel to and From Airports

Ground access refers to travel to or from airports via external transportation systems and includes public and private transportation services and private automobiles. *ACRP Report 4: Ground Access to Major Airports by Public Transportation*, which provides resources to improve

Table 2.   Typology examples for intermodal passenger facilities.

Facility Name	Intercity Rail	Intercity Bus	Regional Rail	Regional Bus	Ferry	Function	Context	Activity Generator
Charlotte Transportation Center			√	√		Central	Urban	Business district, event center
Cincinnati Northside Transit Center				√		Subregional	Suburban	None
Denver Union Station	√	√	√	√		Central	Urban	Business district
Fort Lauderdale Downtown Mobility Hub	√			√		Subregional	Urban	Business district, campus
Hoboken Terminal			√	√	√	Subregional	Dense urban	Business district
Indianapolis Julia M. Carson Transit Center				√		Central	Urban	Business district
Los Angeles Union Station	√	√	√	√		Central	Urban	Business district
North Nashville Transit Center				√		Neighborhood	Urban	None
Rio Metro Los Lunas Station			√			Subregional	Rural	None
San Francisco Ferry Terminal			√	√	√	Central	Dense urban	Business district
San Francisco Transbay Terminal		√		√		Subregional	Dense urban	Business district
San Jose Diridon Station	√	√	√	√		Central	Urban	Business district
Seattle Colman Dock				√	√	Subregional	Urban	Business district
Washington Union Station	√	√	√	√		Central	Dense urban	Business district, major attraction

the quality of public transportation services at U.S. airports, defines public transportation access as via rail, bus, and shared-ride vans, but not single-party limousines, courtesy shuttles, or charter operations (Coogan et al. 2008).

While most of the primary and medium-hub airports in the United States offer some public transportation access as defined previously, connecting to such services varies. In some airports, individuals can walk to a nearby rail station, some require connections via bus or rail, and others offer curbside bus services. Public transportation use at most U.S. airports is relatively low, with only some seeing larger market shares. *ACRP Report 4* analyzed 2005 origin–destination data to rank the volume of public transportation use at 27 U.S. airports, showing a range of 200,000 to 2,200,000 annual users. Just six of the 27 top airports had ground access market shares of at least 15% (San Francisco, New York JFK, Boston, Reagan National, Oakland, and New Orleans). Of these, San Francisco, New York JFK, Reagan National, and Oakland provide direct rail connections. Boston provides shuttle service to nearby rail (Silver Line bus service between Logan Airport and South Station began in 2009), and New Orleans has no rail service.

Entering and Traveling Through Airports

The TSA manages airside access to U.S. airports. (It is worth noting that Amtrak also screens baggage on long-distance routes.) Individuals connecting from a domestic flight to another flight who remain in secured areas do not need additional screening. Except for international flights from airports with preclearance facilities (in 2024, preclearance was available in Ireland, Aruba, Bermuda, United Arab Emirates, Bahamas, and Canada), individuals arriving in the United States must go through immigration, and after retrieving checked baggage, must pass through customs. Individuals with checked bags connecting to another flight must recheck their bags and proceed through TSA screening.

Applying Station Typologies – Planning Examples

This section discusses examples applicable to all intermodal passenger facilities. The process of planning new intermodal passenger facilities or renovating existing facilities involves extensive coordination. For complex projects, the timeline can be lengthy, making it difficult to anticipate how travel will change. The following are examples of how some entities use typologies as part of the planning process.

A Typology Framework for Station Area Planning in the Netherlands

In the Netherlands, ProRail is responsible for maintaining and extending the Dutch National Railway network. The station area planning process for developing new or redeveloping existing stations considers the station's urban context, available mobility options, and relationship to the larger rail transport network. Working with all stakeholders, the process developed by Goudappel Groep B.V. asks participants to characterize the current station area and to share their aspirations for its redevelopment. Figure 5 illustrates the relationship of the station's function (network), urban areas (anchors), mobility (ground access), and location (context), which are key components used in the redevelopment of Leiden Station.

Because each station differs and each stakeholder community is unique, planners use this framework to establish collective understandings of current conditions and the desired future state. A key goal of planners is to build/rebuild intermodal passenger facilities that work well for all user groups (residents, visitors, and travelers—symbolized by the people at the center of the figure) who can enjoy the station as both a hub for mobility and for non-mobility activities. This might result in prioritizing walking and bicycling over driving as a station access mode, increasing security features, or improving ease of transferring between modes.

Using a Typology to Support Access Goals in Boston, Massachusetts

In 2020, the Massachusetts Department of Transportation (MassDOT) and the Massachusetts Bay Transportation Authority (MBTA) completed a station access study with three main goals. The first was to improve its customer focus by providing a safe, positive, and reliable customer experience. The second was to improve business performance by increasing transit ridership, increasing fiscal resiliency, and managing costs. The third goal was to improve social and environmental stewardship to reshape historical social inequities and combat climate change

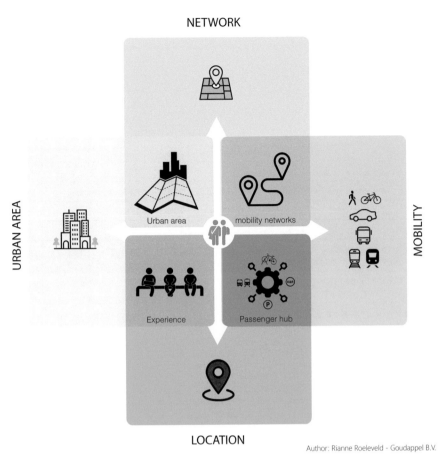

Source: Goudappel Groep B.V.

Author: Rianne Roeleveld - Goudappel B.V.

Figure 5.   Planning process for Leiden Station redevelopment in the Netherlands.

(MassDOT and MBTA 2020a). The study included a typology for rapid transit service and for commuter rail that established station types based on context, magnitude of bus transfers, and mode of access (excluding buses), as presented in Table 3.

Applying Typology Principles to a Major Project: The Port Authority Bus Terminal Renovation

The Port Authority of New York and New Jersey (PANYNJ) issued a draft environmental impact statement (DEIS) for its bus terminal replacement project in February 2024. This complex multiyear project will transform the user experience for customers, tenants, bus operators, and others and revitalize the surrounding areas of Manhattan. This project is in a dense urban business district and will replace the existing terminal. As part of area revitalization efforts and to help finance the cost, the project includes commercial development in new towers. At its core, however, the project will dramatically increase intermodal capacity. According to the DEIS, the project has the following goals:

- Improve bus operations through direct linkages to the Lincoln Tunnel and to bus storage and staging areas.
- Improve the customer experience in the terminal with amenities and through safety and security.

Table 3. MBTA station typology and mode shares.

Primary Service	Station Type	Number of Stations	Magnitude of Bus Transfers	Mode Share (Except Bus Transfers)			
				Walk or Bike	Drive Alone	Carpool	Dropped Off
Rapid transit	Core	68	None to moderate	95%	1%	0%	4%
	Neighborhood	68	None to moderate	87%	6%	1%	6%
	Regional	26	High	83%	7%	1%	9%
Commuter rail	Town centers	46	None	38%	43%	4%	15%
	Neighborhood	29	None to low	70%	21%	2%	7%
	Urban centers	14	Low	31%	44%	3%	22%
	Regional park-and-rides	17	None	8%	68%	4%	20%
	Local park-and-rides	26	None	15%	62%	5%	18%

Source: MassDOT and MBTA (2020a)

- Provide seamless passenger accessibility within the facility, strengthening transit connections and supporting bicycling and walking.
- Strive to achieve consistency with local and regional land use plans and initiatives through new civic spaces, as well as integration with the surrounding neighborhood and with West Midtown development projects.
- Optimize life-cycle costs through phased construction and other approaches.
- Reduce the impacts of bus services on the built and natural environment by reducing bus idling, unnecessary bus circulation, and local traffic impacts (Federal Transit Administration and Port Authority of NY & NJ 2024).

CHAPTER 5

Planning and Decision-Making Framework

Introduction

This chapter outlines a framework for intermodal passenger facility planning and decision-making, taking into accounts different contexts, current trends, and potential uncertainties. It introduces 10 planning and decision-making categories with steps and considerations for implementing new or renovation projects and for ongoing operations. It introduces the complete trip concept and discusses how well-designed and well-managed intermodal passenger facilities can support seamless travel. It includes an example of how to use the typology and apply the framework to managing pickups and drop-offs and discusses other key elements of passenger facilities.

Categories of Planning and Decision-Making

Intermodal passenger facility planning and decision-making can be organized into 10 general categories:

- Governance and partnerships (see Chapter 7).
- Funding and finance (see Chapter 8).
- Permitting and regulations.
- Site planning and design.
- Equity and inclusion.
- Operations and maintenance.
- Safety and security.
- User experience.
- Data and information needs (see Chapter 6).
- Technology and systems.

Each intermodal passenger facility project is unique, and decisions should reflect the context and goals for that facility. Based on interviews with facility planners and owners, modal operators, and industry experts, certain important steps and considerations apply to most facilities. Table 4 highlights key steps and considerations for each planning category.

Supporting the Complete Trip and User Experience

According to U.S. DOT's complete trip definition, a trip is complete when an individual traveler can execute every part of their trip from origin to destination regardless of location, income, or disability (U.S. Department of Transportation, n.d.). [The U.S. DOT Intelligent Transportation Systems Joint Program Office (ITS JPO) directs the Complete Trip – ITS4US Deployment Program, a partnership among FTA, FHWA, and Office of the Secretary of Transportation (OST).

Table 4. Selected steps and decision-making considerations by planning category.

Planning Category	Selected Steps and Decision-Making Considerations
Governance and Partnerships	• Identify and map stakeholders • Select from available models of governance • Select project delivery method • Define and assign roles and responsibilities • Define business partnerships, including data-sharing agreements
Funding and Finance	• Select from available funding and financing methods • Formalize applicable development partnerships • Leverage and capture value from surrounding development • Establish revenue-generating partnerships
Permitting and Regulations	• Identify and map stakeholders early in the process • Understand regulatory constraints • Work to make permitting process inclusive and equitable
Site Planning and Design	• Plan and design to maximize seamless modal transfers • Prioritize the user experience • Consult TCQSM • Design ground access connections well, particularly for passenger pickups • Integrate art and other design features
Equity and Inclusion	• Identify and include stakeholders in planning • Serve all travelers, including those with limited English proficiency and those with disabilities • Accommodate needs of intercity bus travelers
Operations and Maintenance	• Dedicate resources for ongoing maintenance, including addressing maintenance backlogs • Clarify roles and responsibilities using RACI (responsible, accountable, consulted, informed) matrix • Cross-train staff to respond to changes in demand and to emergencies within and outside facility
Safety and Security	• Define responsibilities and training needs • Establish and maintain partnership agreements, including with local law enforcement • Consider ways to manage access (open to all or limited to ticketed passengers)
User Experience	• Use complete-trip approach • Design sustainable wayfinding system • Provide adequate staff to assist passengers • Consider needs of employees working for modal provider and within the facility
Data and Information Needs	• Establish plans for recurring data collection, data stewardship, and data sharing • Include data reporting requirements in partnership agreements • Use data to plan for demand fluctuations and trend analyses
Technology and Systems	• Formalize and update technology policies • Provide ongoing training and maintenance • Work with partners on MaaS strategy

The program provides funding to communities to showcase innovative business partnerships, technologies, and practices that promote independent mobility for all travelers.] Successfully executing each part of the complete trip is a minimum. An optimum trip is seamless, easy, and comfortable, without gaps, barriers, unreliable connections, or inefficient or circuitous travel options. Intermodal passenger facilities can help users achieve this optimum trip by emphasizing the user experience, which includes entering, using, and exiting the facility.

DOT's complete trip, illustrated in Figure 6, involves multiple steps, including trip planning, navigating outdoor spaces, crossing intersections, boarding/using vehicles, paying fares or fees, transferring, transitioning to and from indoor spaces (and navigating them), and making further connections.

Table 5 demonstrates how an intermodal passenger facility supports each complete trip segment. Next is a discussion of:

- Public information for trip planning;
- Wayfinding for outdoor and indoor navigation;
- Design for connections, modal transfers, and street crossings; and
- Staffing, training, and contingency planning for indoor navigation.

Source: U.S. Department of Transportation, n.d.

Figure 6.   U.S. DOT's complete trip.

Table 5. How an intermodal passenger facility supports the complete trip.

Complete Trip Segment	Role of the Intermodal Facility
Trip planning	▪ Provides information on websites and other places welcoming customers and explaining how to travel to/from the facility and how to navigate it
Outdoor navigation	▪ Orients customers and others arriving at or leaving the facility by explaining travel options, navigation within the facility, and orientation to surrounding community
Boarding/using vehicles	▪ Offers clear directions to available parking, pickup and drop-off zones, or other ground transportation services ▪ Prioritizes pedestrian safety and navigation ▪ Ensures adequate staffing is available during surge periods
Vehicle/mode transfers/ payments	▪ Sizes passenger boarding and alighting zones adequately, particularly for passengers with luggage ▪ Incorporates all modes, including intercity bus ▪ Ensures that all customers have access to amenities and different fare payment options ▪ Considers the needs of passengers with disabilities and those with limited English proficiency
Indoor/outdoor transition	▪ Ensures that horizontal circulation, vertical circulation, entrances, and exits are properly sized with clear wayfinding
Indoor navigation and use	▪ Provides attractive, comfortable, and well-illuminated spaces with inviting customer amenities
Connecting to/completing trip segments	▪ Facilitates safe, smooth intermodal transfers minimizing travel distances, offering needed assistance, and providing clear wayfinding

Public Information Trip Planning

Many customers who directly plan trips visit websites—either provider sites or travel sites. Such websites often include limited information about the intermodal passenger facility the customer will be using, leaving that part of trip planning to the customer. Facility owners can ensure that their websites offer clear and comprehensive information on what to expect when using their facility, what amenities are available and where they are located, and how to seek additional information. For example, customers may wish to know how to connect to Wi-Fi, whether Internet access is free, and where to charge devices.

Facility owners can work with partners (modal providers, local governments, nearby businesses, and local community groups) to ensure that information about traveling to/from the facility is current and easily accessible. They can also offer multiple channels for obtaining information and can be prepared to assist visitors using the facility, either with volunteer ambassadors or employees.

Wayfinding for Outdoor and Indoor Navigation

Wayfinding systems help people understand places and find destinations efficiently. By contrast, getting lost is almost always a negative experience and one that can have wider impacts. Some key principles of wayfinding include distinguishing places from one another to avoid confusion, limiting navigation choices, maximizing lines of sight, and offering simple and usable maps. As certain intermodal passenger facilities become larger, particularly airport terminals, wayfinding systems need clear information and signs placed at decision points to keep people on the proper path. This includes potential points of confusion where a traveler might make an incorrect choice based on broad categories such as ground transportation or potentially confusing terminology such as "app pickup" for ridehailing/TNCs. Furthermore, not all customers have sufficient language proficiency to understand signs in English. Having information in other languages

Transit Wayfinding Principles in Boston, Massachusetts

The MBTA Station Access Playbook (MassDOT and MBTA 2020b) includes the following wayfinding guidance for facilitating connections to other modes and other destinations:

- Use symbology, letters, or numerals for each station access point and integrate them into station signage.
- Work with municipalities to incorporate more context-specific wayfinding in station areas.
- Develop standards for temporary wayfinding measures for special events and for service disruptions.
- Prioritize where passengers make multimodal connections, particularly when connecting buses are not within the station.
- Integrate key destination wayfinding.
- Be consistent in design and tone.
- Provide information that is easily understood by visitors, new transit riders, and everyday commuters.

(MassDOT and MBTA 2020b).

and using graphics with universal symbols can help those with limited English proficiency. For more information, see *ACRP Research Report 177* (Harding et al. 2017).

Designing for Connections, Modal Transfers, and Street Crossings

A barrier-free seamless travel experience begins with good design, including the design of the physical space and the placement of elements within the space. Examples include limiting the distance that customers must travel and integrating moving walkways when distances are farther apart. [See TCQSM (Kittelson & Associates, Inc., et al. 2013).]

Prioritizing the user experience also means applying inclusive design principles that help all customers. For example, while the proliferation of smartphones has enabled many customers to plan, reserve, and pay for travel and to better navigate spaces, particularly outdoors, not all customers use technology for these purposes. Furthermore, not all customers have sufficient language proficiency to understand signs in English. Having information in other languages, using graphics with universal symbols, and offering alternative ways to pay for travel can help to address these challenges.

In addition, while older adults may speak English and may be perfectly comfortable with technology while traveling, they may still face challenges walking longer distances or they may be able to walk without difficulty but lack the confidence to navigate large unfamiliar spaces. Passengers with disabilities regularly encounter barriers or challenges even when facilities are designed to comply with the ADA. Examples include inoperable elevators or poorly placed accessibility features, missing or confusing signs, or curb ramps that do not align with street crossings. Universal design principles employed in the design and operation of intermodal passenger facilities can address many of these concerns by ensuring that facility features work for everyone (Harding et al. 2017). See TCQSM discussion for information on designing platforms, walkways, and vertical circulation areas.

Integrating Art into Intermodal Passenger Facilities

The introduction of documented artworks into transportation environments in the United States dates to the late 1800s, with a tradition of government programs funding art in public facilities that began in the mid-1930s (Yamamoto 2018). The U.S. DOT has been funding and supporting artworks in transportation projects since 1977, including in public transit. In 2011, APTA published a recommended practice, *Why Design Matters for Transit* (APTA 2011), and updated it in 2013. That same year, APTA also published *Best Practices for Integrating Art into Capital Projects*, which addresses the importance of art program development at the earliest stages of a capital project's development. The report also notes that art must be maintained and that ongoing programs should introduce the public to art installed on the transit system (APTA 2013). Customers place a high value on the overall quality of differentiated yet deeply integrated experiences (Yamamoto 2018). The presence of art and good user-centered facility design are integral to the user experience and can also serve to engage community stakeholders in intermodal passenger facility projects.

Staffing, Training, and Contingency Planning for Connecting and Completing Trip Segments

While the sizing of spaces and circulation elements and the design of wayfinding systems are essential elements of the design process, staffing, training, and management of facility personnel are essential to supporting the complete trip. For example, travel delays are common at facilities that serve intercity travel. While individual carriers or providers are responsible for rearranging travel, sufficiently sized waiting areas and circulation spaces can mitigate crowd surges.

Training, Cross-Training, and Contingency Planning

Customer-facing employees who work at intermodal passenger facilities or for providers receive training appropriate to their assigned duties, and cross-training helps employees assume other roles when required. Cross-training is increasingly needed for working with homeless individuals, responding to severe weather events, and responding to emergencies.

In transit, cross-agency training for public transportation employees can provide important staff capacity building and can support mutual understanding. Bay Area Rapid Transit (BART) includes a ride-along experience with transit police as part of its 30-day orientation for case management staff, who are partnered with transit officers to promote cross-discipline understanding (Zapata et al. 2024). This is particularly useful for working with homeless individuals or people who are in distress. As part of its ongoing efforts to change practices for interacting with unsheltered populations, the Metropolitan Atlanta Regional Transit Authority (MARTA) has invested in cross-training its outreach, customer service, and some operational staff in cultural awareness and de-escalation skills (Zapata et al. 2024).

Integrating Art and Local History into Cincinnati's Northside Transit Center

In the development of new transit on Cincinnati's north side, the Southwest Ohio Regional Transit Authority (SORTA) and its planning team worked to ensure that the facility reflected the surrounding community's strong connection to the arts. The new center includes nine bus shelters, each with a pillar displaying route information on one side and featuring local historical information on the reverse. The community contributed facts and stories to the project. SORTA also held an art competition and placed the winning designs on the pillars.

According to *NCHRP Research Report 970: Mainstreaming System Resilience Concepts into Transportation Agencies: A Guide*, transportation agencies should ensure that decision-making processes and employee availability can survive major disruptions. A continuous order of operations plan (COOP) outlines the hierarchy of decision-making if key leadership is unable to make decisions (Dorney et al. 2021). The report suggests that the COOP include contingency procedures for different events based on frequency, duration, and impact.

Intermodal passenger facility owners can design and distribute emergency response procedure flip charts for events such as medical emergencies, tornadoes, power outages, chemical or biohazard spills, and fires.

Applying the Typology and Planning Categories for Managing Pickups and Drop-Offs

Ground access is an integral part of the complete trip for intermodal travel and for those arriving by car or bus; this means pickups and drop-offs. This section uses this important topic to demonstrate how to use the typology and planning categories for making decisions about managing pickups and drop-offs. It includes use cases and suggested guidance.

Typology Categories and Applications for Ground Access

Passenger pickups and drop-offs are integral to all large- and medium-hub airports. At intermodal ground passenger facilities, managing pickups and drop-offs is typically a higher priority at central and subregional facilities and can also be a priority at certain stations, terminals, and docks. The extent of planning required depends on the volume of intercity travel, development anchors, and site configuration.

Planning Considerations for Pickup and Drop-Off Management

Table 6 illustrates how the planning framework applies to ground access and includes steps and planning considerations.

It is not common for the facility owner to have control of the adjacent curb and street. While facilities with internal circulation roadways or those that control the curb can apply methods used at airports, when the curb space or street is separately owned, data management agreements and related partnership agreements help to improve coordination and clarify responsibilities. In addition, on-site supervision may be necessary to manage operations, protect vulnerable users, and ensure adjacent traffic flow. Facilities that accommodate pickup/drop-off activities on land they control (either on streets they control or off-street) may also need to devote staff resources to managing surges in demand.

Table 6. Planning categories and considerations for pickup and drop-off management.

Category	Considerations
Governance and Partnerships	▪ Establish clear regulatory frameworks and partnership agreements with operators
Funding and Finance	▪ Invest in expanded circulation areas to provide funding for staffing to manage operations ▪ Seek revenues from private entities through partnership agreements
Permitting and Regulations	▪ Understand what is permissible in governing regulations (state, local) ▪ Executing data-sharing agreement during permitting
Site Planning and Design	▪ Prioritize transit modes over passenger vehicles to not disrupt or inconvenience pedestrian, bike, or transit access ▪ Integrate on-site pickup and drop-off zones ▪ Separate commercial and private passenger vehicles for pickups ▪ Consider cell-phone lots for private vehicles and geofenced meeting areas for ridehailing/TNCs
Equity and Inclusion	▪ Prioritize siting and availability of lowest-cost transportation modes ▪ Ensure that signage and wayfinding maximizes use of universal symbols
Operations and Maintenance	▪ Include resources to assign staff during surges ▪ Rework space allocation based on data collected and lessons learned
Safety and Security	▪ Prioritize pedestrian safety in design of circulation areas, including providing clear sight lines ▪ Provide secure waiting areas, particularly during times of low activity and staff
User Experience	▪ Prioritize pedestrian circulation ▪ Provide consistent and clear wayfinding ▪ Offer well-lighted, safe, and secure waiting areas
Data and Information Needs	▪ Require data sharing when executing partnership agreements ▪ Collect and analyzing data to modify operations plans based on demand and lessons learned
Technology and Systems	▪ Evaluate and deploy curb management tools ▪ Ensure that any real-time signage integrates modes available and offers clear directions

Establishing a Curb Access Hierarchy at MBTA Stations

As part of its station access planning efforts with MassDOT, the MBTA established modal hierarchies for its rapid transit and commuter rail stations. Table 7 shows a summary of prioritizing curb access by mode.

Management of Curb Spaces and Other Rights-of-Way with Advanced Technology

Intermodal passenger facility owners and the government agencies that manage the public rights-of-way that serve them are increasingly relying on connected vehicle (CV) technology and other systems to exchange information, whether between systems or between people. *NCHRP Web Only Document 340: Dynamic Curbside Management: Keeping Pace with New and Emerging Mobility and Technology in the Public Right-of-Way* (Mitman et al. 2022) offers a framework for planning and managing the curb with a focus on using data and systems for improving performance and efficiency. The growth in AVs and CVs and associated advancements in technology and CV communications systems offer potential benefits to improving efficiency and system performance.

The *ITE Curbside Management Practitioners Guide* (Institute of Transportation Engineers 2019) includes suggestions for curb space allocation policy and implementation and presents a framework and toolbox for analyzing and optimizing curb space. This guide includes planning and implementation considerations, policy development, prioritization, available tools and treatments, and evaluation metrics

The International Transport Forum Report, *The Shared-Use City: Managing the Curb* (International Transport Forum 2018) discusses the street design and pricing implications of a large-scale introduction of ridehailing/TNCs and other innovative mobility options in urban settings. It looks at the potential for a shift away from a model of the use of curb space focused on street parking to one that makes more flexible use of curb space for pickup and drop-off zones for passengers and freight. The study presents the results of quantitative modeling of alternative curb-use scenarios and discusses their relative efficiency, how flexible curb space contributes to wider policy objectives, and implications on city revenues.

Table 7. Curb access hierarchy guidance for MBTA stations.

Curb Use	Hierarchy, Placement, or Role
Paratransit	Closest access to station entrance.
Transit use (bus)	Second closest access if it has been determined that bus connection will directly access the station. Considering feasibility of route deviation, this is not always possible. If buses directly access the station, the stop should be closer to the station than the nearest parking space. Regardless of location, design bus stops to avoid conflicts with other modes to ensure easy curb access.
Private shuttles	Provide space for shuttles in scale with capacity and demand. Designated space is warranted in high-volume contexts where shuttles serve as a large first-/last-mile resource. In lower-volume locations, mixing with other modes (besides paratransit or transit) is acceptable.
Bike access and parking	The location and quality of bike parking is essential to increasing bike access systemwide. Follow standards for placement and type.
Micromobility parking	Provide easy access to the station entrance (closer than the nearest parking space) without interfering with pedestrian, paratransit, or bus movements. Group and make visible to increase usage.
Pickup/drop-off (personal and taxi/ridehailing)	"At high-volume stations, if room is available, ideally separate [taxis and ridehailing services from] personal vehicle loading. Can combine these in low-volume stations" (MassDOT and MBTA 2020a).

Source: MassDOT and MBTA (2020a)

Applicable Information and Lessons Learned from Airport Curb Management Strategies

ACRP Research Report 266: Airport Curbside and Terminal Area Roadway Operations: New Analysis and Strategies, Second Edition (InterVISTAS Consulting, Inc., forthcoming) offers information on a cohesive approach to analyzing traffic operations on airport curbside and terminal area roadways. The previous edition was published in 2010 as *ACRP Report 40: Airport and Terminal Area Roadway Operations* (LeighFisher 2010). *ACRP Research Report 266* also covers sustainability, customer service, enforcement, TNCs, and peer-to-peer car rentals, and also considers anticipated services such as automated vehicles.

ACRP Research Report 266 uses the collective experiences of airport operators to assist others in improving the passenger pickup process, including better matching of arriving passengers with scheduled and demand-response transportation services. Airports with noteworthy remote (i.e., off the terminal frontage) ridehailing pickup operations include Los Angeles International Airport (LAX) and LaGuardia Airport (LGA). Both rely on application programming interface (API) data to monitor and collect information on arriving and departing TNC trips. Some innovative curb management strategies developed at airports can be applied to other ground transportation facilities in the following ways:

- **Enforcement:** Use both sworn and civilian officers for traffic management.
- **Signage:** Provide clear wayfinding signage for customers entering and exiting the facility and for all vehicle operators (bus operators, taxi or TNC drivers, private vehicle drivers).
- **Surge management:** Accommodate customer surges from the arrival of a ferry or intercity train by integrating schedules, tracking real-time arrivals, and adequately staffing periods of peak demand.
- **Transit promotion:** Prioritize curb access to encourage higher-occupancy shared transportation modes by reserving zones using design features and active curb management strategies.
- **Trip planning:** Work to integrate information on available landside modes (transit, bikeshare, ridehailing, private shuttles) with trip planning applications and on intermodal passenger facility websites.

Los Angeles International Airport TNC Monitoring Program

At LAX, an API transmits a unique vehicle identifier, arrival time, time and location of passenger pickup, time of exit, time and location of drop-off, trip duration, and passenger wait time. LAX operators use these data to establish possible airport access fees, improve curb management, and plan for future capital improvements.

Tracking FHVs at the New York Region's Airports

The City of New York Taxi and Limousine Commission (TLC) oversees taxis and FHVs. The TLC gathers data from taxis via electronic meters in each vehicle that capture pickup and drop-off dates, times, locations, distances, fares, rate and payment types, and driver-reported passenger counts. FHVs share data via APIs and via FHV bases (entities licensed to accept and dispatch trip requests) that capture vehicle license, pickup date, time, and location identifier. Having these data available enables trend analysis, showing how FHV use increased between 2016 and 2018, which in turn led to allocating more space allocated for FHV pickup and staging. (See Figure 7.)

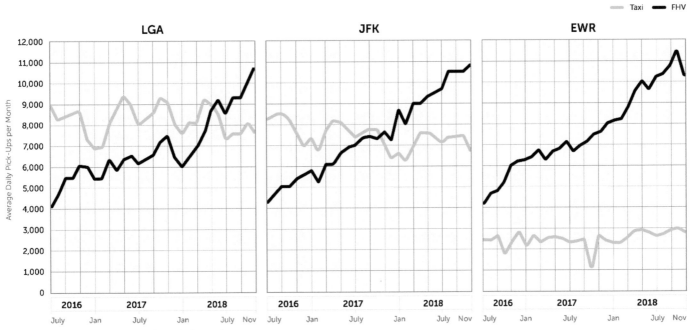

Source: NYC Taxi and Limousine Commission, n.d.

Figure 7.   Monthly FHV and taxi pickups at New York's airports (2016–2018).

Privately Owned Vehicles

Whether for pickup or drop-off or for parking, the use of privately owned vehicles is an essential and often dominant travel mode. While many well-designed parking strategies are available, managing private drivers arriving to pick up and drop off passengers is far more challenging, often necessitating operations staff to manage the flow of vehicles (as frequently seen at airports).

CHAPTER 6

Data and Information Needs

Introduction

Intermodal passenger facility owners and providers rely on data to understand daily operations and trends and flag issues requiring attention. The quality of available data and the use of data to make decisions varies, in part due to the lack of established practices around data management and limited understanding of how to leverage insights obtained from data. Data-driven decision-making can enable those managing and operating intermodal passenger facilities to better adapt to change. This chapter explains how to plan and manage data collection, including methods, approaches to data stewardship, and the use of data-sharing agreements. It describes new sources of data and discusses data used for different travel modes, and it provides examples of using technology and systems to measure facility performance.

Data Collection Planning and Management

Data collection and management plans typically have the following elements:

- Purpose.
- Methods.
- Data stewardship.
- Staff responsibilities.

Purpose

Intermodal passenger facilities may include multiple modes of transportation, each with their own set of unique data outputs. Before deciding what data to collect, owners and operators should identify what information is important to understand, what decisions need to be made with those data, and what analyses will be performed.

Methods

Data collection can occur in different ways. With new technology and mobility options available, the transportation industry is relying less on manual data collection and more on automatic and continuous data collection. When possible, data should be made available without restrictions in order to simplify collection and analysis. This facilitates connections to open-source (unrestricted) APIs that enable computer programs to communicate directly.

Integrating New Methods

Integrating new information with existing data sources and data management processes can be challenging. This integration may require updating prior methods of data collection while still maintaining key performance indicators (KPIs) already in use.

A comprehensive data integration plan typically includes timelines, data details, validation, processes, and needed changes to database management and architecture. Staff should understand how to use and interpret new data sources and understand data limitations. For example, if an intermodal passenger facility previously relied on a regional transit operator to send monthly summaries of daily boarding and alighting at each stop and route serving the intermodal passenger facility, related KPIs should be updated to connect to the transit API providing real-time General Transit Feed Specification (GTFS) data. Improved real-time data could help facility operators respond to variations in demand and better manage staffing. Any methods of manual data collection should also include plans for updates on a recurring basis.

Data Stewardship

Data stewardship is a set of policies and practices for ensuring that data are well managed. Data stewardship includes collecting, storing, sharing, archiving, and deleting data. It helps to support accuracy and trust by creating a structure for staff and other stakeholders to access data for planning, analysis, summary, and reporting purposes. In defining an approach to data stewardship, the following topics should be explored:

- Privacy and security of incoming data.
- Policies to secure private personal information.
- Capabilities of data storage.
- Procedure for scraping, validating, and cleaning data to convert to usable format.

As new data sources expand and become more available, data stewardship helps to ensure that data can be processed and that generated reports are accurate. Moreover, as the measurement of facility use increasingly relies on real-time data and access to provider APIs, effective data stewardship will become more critical for responding quickly and effectively to changes and incidents.

Data Management Principles Checklist

NCFRP Web Resource 49: Understanding and Using New Data Sources to Address Urban and Metropolitan Freight Challenges suggests the following checklist of data management principles, which are applicable to intermodal passenger facilities:

- Does your agency retain and store information that it believes will be valuable for research or decision-making in the future?
- Does your agency prescribe or otherwise require how geographic or location-related attributes are recorded and used?
- Is your agency's data frequently refreshed, and will it be updated or cleaned in the future?
- Have the data themselves been explained or described logically so that the data are understood and used appropriately?
- Are the data easy to find by those who need to use them?
- Are the data openly available, and are any restrictions clearly stated and justified?

The web resource suggests that answering these questions can help determine if the principle of data management applies and suggests possible actions or tools to aid in implementation (*CPCS and Ludlow* 2019).

NCFRP Web Resource 49: Understanding and Using New Data Sources to Address Urban and Metropolitan Freight Challenges includes a discussion of data stewardship and principles, including transparency and openness, purpose specification, data minimization, retention and use limitation, data quality and accuracy, accountability, security, and data management (CPCS and Ludlow 2019).

Staff Responsibilities

An effective data collection and management plan should outline the staffing resources and capabilities to execute the plan. If the plan involves use of multiple open-source APIs for collecting real-time data, hiring staff trained to write code and maintain API connections is essential to ensure collected data remains usable. Business intelligence dashboards are real-time information management tools that provide a visual representation of real-time data in support of data-driven decision-making (Patel 2023). Examples include PowerBI and Tableau.

Data Sharing

Intermodal passenger facility owners are in a unique position to be both generators of sharable data and recipients of external data. Expanded access to data may help facility owners make less-siloed operational decisions with greater efficiency and visibility. Connectivity between modes can be optimized, supply and demand patterns can be better understood, and planning and operations can be undertaken more effectively. However, there are barriers to data sharing, such as privacy and security concerns, concerns within for-profit industries about competition, and cost considerations since cleaning, refining, and maintaining big data is expensive. Data-sharing agreements can help to alleviate some of these barriers.

Agreements to use or share data are formal contracts that clearly document the shared data and the parameters for data use. Agreements protect the agency or organization providing the data, the data subjects, and the entity receiving the information. These agreements confirm who is authorized to use the data, what the purpose of the use is, and that the data transfer is compliant with legal and ethical standards.

To access and harness big data sources for operations and service delivery analysis, facility owners may engage mobility providers, data gatherers and aggregators, and other agencies. Data-sharing agreements should be clear and offer a reasonable degree of specificity about the purpose of the collected or acquired data, should identify which data points are critical, and should specify the granularity needed to meet objectives.

Understanding the purpose of the compiled data is paramount. This helps to structure agreements that allow facility planners and operators to gather and store the most helpful data without paying to store large volumes of information that do not add value.

Elements of Data-Sharing Agreements

At a minimum, data-sharing agreements should include the following:

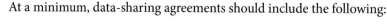

- A detailed project description.
- Terms of use, including details on use, re-use, disclosure, and any exclusions or limitations.
- Roles and responsibilities of each party regarding:
  - Data ownership, collection, maintenance and updates, storage, archiving, and disposal.
- Method and frequency of data transmission.
- Type and quality of data to be shared.
- Security and safeguard measures to ensure privacy of data subjects, including specific requirements about omission of certain types of payment or personally identifiable information as may be required by government entities.

- Agreement duration and circumstances for termination.
- Financial cost of the data sharing.
- General legal provisions, such as dispute resolution, liability, and indemnification.

TCRP Research Report 213: Data Sharing Guidance for Public Transit Agencies—Now and in the Future (Weisbrod et al. 2020) offers quick study results and guidance on sharing agency data and data from others. It also offers suggestions on how to evaluate benefits, costs, and risks.

Data-sharing agreements can specify data-sharing formats. Adopting recognized standards will streamline data management and allow for comparison across facilities and jurisdictions. Developed standards improve access, compatibility, and interoperability. Standards also benefit from privacy and data security. In addition, agencies that have not done so should consider adopting digital policies, which can then be integrated into data-sharing agreements.

New Data Resources

Geolocation technology has made it easier to track people and vehicles. Broad use of geolocation-enabled smartphones has in turn created new industries in data aggregation and analytics, known as big data, and this landscape is rapidly evolving. Private companies and government agencies now employ data scientists to gain meaning from vast amounts of data. The use and potential of artificial intelligence is also rapidly evolving. Machine learning, a subfield of artificial intelligence, enables computers to learn from data without being programmed to do so. Machine learning can be particularly helpful when working with large or complex datasets that require sophisticated analysis to gain usable insights (FasterCapital, n.d.).

Open Data Standards

Open standards enable ongoing and consistent communication of information between devices. Whenever possible, data inputs should follow open standards to facilitate consistent communication of information between devices (Feigon and Murphy 2016) through the GTFS, Mobility Data Specification (MDS), and General Bikeshare Feed Specification (GBFS). Table 8 explains how these standards can be used at intermodal passenger facilities.

Big Data

Big data is a term used to refer to datasets that are too large or complex for traditional data-processing application software to adequately deal with (Franzwa, n.d.). Numerous companies

Table 8. Applicability of open standards to intermodal passenger facilities.

Standard	Applicability to Intermodal Passenger Facilities
General Transit Feed Specification (GTFS)	Integration of schedules into trip planners and digital information systems, tracking of real-time arrivals for curb management, and response to service disruptions.
General Bikeshare Feed Specifications (GBFS)	Integration of bikeshare dock and bicycle locations and availability into trip planning applications and for monitoring.
Mobility Data Standard (MDS)	Tracking of private mobility provider data for owner oversight and monitoring.
Curb Data Specification (CDS)	At airports, the CDS can be used to actively monitor curb activities. At intermodal ground passenger facilities, municipalities that typically have jurisdiction of the curb can adjust pricing and target enforcement activities.

compile, analyze, and sell access to big data, offering information that can support intermodal passenger facility planning. Onboard vehicle-location computers in cars, buses, and trucks, and smartphones provide much of the data. The International Transport Forum's Use of Big Data in Transport Modelling highlights the potential of mobile data to enhance travel modeling and overall decision-making (Willumsen 2021). The paper emphasizes how big data can explain trends and improve travel demand forecasts, particularly for micromobility use (Willumsen 2021).

Appendix B contains information on private companies that compile, repackage, and sell big data for transportation analysis applicable to intermodal passenger facilities.

Mode-Level Data

Modal data and performance measurement are unique to each mode (Margiotta et al. 2017). Recognizing modal differences and working to integrate certain measures is important for better managing intermodal passenger facilities, particularly for analyzing the user experience.

The following discussion notes any available open data standards and offers guidance on how to collect and analyze data for facility planning. Topics discussed are:

- Public buses and shuttles,
- Ridehailing/TNCs,
- Privately owned vehicles,
- Micromobility (bicycles, scooters, bikesharing, and scooter sharing),
- Carsharing,
- Pedestrian data, and
- EV infrastructure.

 The findings of NCHRP Project 08-36/Task 131, "Transportation Data Integration to Develop Planning Performance Measures," were published in 2017 by AASHTO as a report and slide presentation. The study found that measures of mobility were shifting to consider how individuals experience the transportation system for complete trips, and that modal performance measures are unique to each mode. The study also noted the need for data on movements at the individual level to support true multimodal performance measurement (Margiotta et al. 2017).

Public Buses and Shuttles

GTFS feeds can be integrated with real-time information throughout an intermodal passenger facility. GTFS data can support the following facility performance measures:

- Number of unique transit routes serving the facility, including fixed-route and demand-response services.
- Fixed-route headways throughout each service day.
- Timetable connections with other scheduled mobility services.
- Actual location of buses and arrival times.

GTFS data can also be used for locating and sizing bus loading/unloading zones, managing bus ingress and egress, coordinating among providers, and understanding the overall operating envelope, including when to assign staff to manage times of high demand.

Many additional transit performance measures are available. [See TCQSM (Kittelson & Associates, Inc., et al. 2013).]

 TCRP Research Report 235: Improving Access and Management of Public Transit ITS Data (EBP et al. 2022) proposes a structure for storing data from bus and rail intelligent transportation systems (ITSs). It also describes how that data structure can facilitate a process by which transit agencies can receive ITS data from vendors, organize and validate the data, and use the data to calculate KPIs to improve transit system operations. To support that process, the report describes procedures that transit agencies, researchers, and consultants can use to develop tools to transform, validate, and analyze ITS data using the data structure.

Ridehailing/TNCs

There are no universal data specifications for ridehailing (services provided by taxis or TNCs). The amount of data shared with government agencies is a function of disparate individual licensing agreements. A universal data specification is needed, particularly given the challenges of managing multiple providers picking up passengers. In locations where such data are available or where companies agree to share information as a condition of access, the way data is collected and shared also differs. Data can be used for space allocation and daily operations, including for TNC and taxi loading zones, pre-loading zones (e.g., taxi stacks), and staging lots (Curtis et al. 2019).

Privately Owned Vehicles

Collecting traffic vehicle volume data is a mainstay of transportation planning. Advanced technologies that count and classify vehicles, such as traffic cameras and license plate readers (LPRs), are a source of reliable and continuous vehicle data. Traffic cameras placed at intersections can collect data and adjust signal timing in response to demand or incidents. In most instances, the technology is under the purview of a local, regional, or state transportation agency. While most intermodal passenger facility operators may not currently participate in traffic operations management, some participation may be beneficial. For example, sharing schedules for modes served, coordinating events, or participating in incident management planning can be helpful when surges in demand could require signal timing adjustments or deployment of personnel to alleviate congestion.

LPR Technology

LPRs are used for tolling, parking management, and curb management. LPR data can help to allocate parking spots by category, set time limits, and automate parking payments. LPRs can replace or enhance parking control systems and can facilitate cashless and barrier-less tolling for facility access by commercial vehicles. [See TCRP Research Report 235 (EBP et al. 2022).]

Measuring Landside Access at Airports

Reliable data on modes used to travel to or from airports are limited. *ACRP Report 4: Ground Access to Major Airports by Public Transportation* noted that fewer than 20 U.S. airport operators regularly conduct passenger surveys that compile this information and noted the significant effort and cost to plan and conduct surveys and analyze results (Coogan et al. 2008).

ACRP Report 266: Airport Roadway Analysis and Curbside Congestion Mitigation Strategies (InterVISTAS Consulting, Inc., forthcoming) noted that information about the number and distribution of arriving and departing passengers by airport, hour, day, or season is not readily available. It stressed the importance of collecting such data and conducting periodic surveys, particularly to monitor trends and for planning improvements (InterVISTAS Consulting, Inc., forthcoming). The same principles apply to other intermodal passenger facilities.

Real-Time Vehicle Tracking

Big data vendors offer services to help facility owners understand real-time vehicle movement and density. Available platforms can monitor speeds and travel times and other travel patterns.

Such data can support reallocation of space or suggest the need for different staffing deployments. For example, at LaGuardia Airport, operations control center staff use Waze and other tools to analyze travel times on pre-identified routes. The tools illustrate the severity of driver delays during peak periods compared to typical conditions (Sam Schwartz 2020).

Micromobility (Bicycles, Scooters, Bikesharing, and Scooter Sharing)

Quantifying micromobility demand and usage can offer intermodal passenger facility owners and others valuable insights on needed infrastructure requirements, curb management, and safety planning. The MDS is a possible resource to inform:

- Placement of bicycle/scooter lanes,
- Size and placement of zones for customers to park e-scooters (drop zones) and demarcation of restricted areas,
- Establishment of vehicle caps,
- Travel speed limits, and
- Distribution of devices (Open Mobility Foundation 2020).

Ongoing NCHRP Project 08-165, "Use of Active Transportation Data in Decision-Making," will ultimately provide informed technical direction to transportation and other professionals on how to identify, access, collect, store, interpret, understand, and apply active transportation data in transportation planning, design, operations and maintenance, safety, performance management, funding, and other decision-making areas.

Important data metrics include temporal trip demand (i.e., peak hour/period trips), connectivity to nearby bicycle infrastructure such as bicycle lanes or bicycle paths, and how demand changes with other modal demand (such as surges that occur when intercity buses, trains, or ferries arrive), which can support analysis of mode of access/egress trends.

Using MDS Data in San Jose

The San Jose Department of Transportation uses the MDS to gather data under its shared micromobility permit regulations, which are specific to e-scooters. San Jose requires scooter-sharing operators within the City of San Jose to provide an automated mechanism to integrate their services with the MDS within 30 days of receiving a permit. The city requires the base data MDS requests as well as additional information such as a maintenance log and response time, including time of request and time of resolution. Vendors must make these data available to city-specified partners.

Compiling and Sharing Bikesharing Data in New York

The New York City Department of Transportation operates Citi Bike in partnership with Lyft. To facilitate access to data on ridership trends and station operations, the Citi Bike website reports historical trip data for the previous 10 years, real-time access to its GBFS feed, and monthly operating reports. The largest stations in the Citi Bike network are at Grand Central Terminal, Penn Station, and the Barclays Center.

Carsharing

For intermodal passenger facilities where carsharing is available on-site or nearby, supply and demand data can be beneficial for facility management. Some agencies have used both MDS and GBFS data specifications to collect and share carsharing data. For example, the city of Seattle tracks the number of participating individuals, size of fleet (gas-powered and electric), supply and location of on- and off-street parking spaces, and other data (Seattle Department of Transportation, n.d.).

Pedestrian Data

Unlike with other modes of transportation, pedestrians are not bound by fixed routes or schedules, making their patterns of movement and use of intermodal passenger facilities more fluid. An ongoing understanding of pedestrian patterns and volumes helps those who plan and operate facilities respond to the needs of passengers and other facility users.

Counting how many people walk and analyzing desire lines can support the management and modification of space allocated to walkways, crosswalks, hallways, waiting areas, gathering spaces, and other places where people walk. In addition, analysis of dwell times—time pedestrians spend waiting at crossings—can aid in reducing congestion and improve safety. Other pedestrian measures to consider are travel distances and time required to walk between connections when transferring since these affect the customer experience.

Pedestrian and Bicyclist Road Safety Audits

FHWA's *Pedestrian and Bicyclist Road Safety Audit (RSA) Guide and Prompt List* provides guidance for auditing pedestrian and bicyclist safety and includes information on safety risks for both modes, the RSA process, necessary data, and the roles and responsibilities of the RSA team. Facility owners looking to examine internal or adjacent sidewalks and streets can use this tool to conduct audits (Goughnour et al. 2020).

EV Infrastructure

The ongoing shift toward EVs may require integration of charging infrastructure at intermodal passenger facilities. EV performance measures may encompass tracking the number of charging stations deployed and their utilization, the adoption rate of EVs, and energy consumption data. (For more information, see Appendix B.)

CHAPTER 7

Governance and Partnerships

Introduction

This chapter introduces intermodal passenger facility governance, using examples from recent projects at airports, ferry terminals, rail stations, and transit centers. It explains the essential elements of governance and the assignment of roles and responsibilities throughout the facility's life cycle. It introduces different models of project delivery and offers an overview of private development partnerships with references to available publications about joint development.

"Governance is the act or process of governing or overseeing the control and direction of something (such as a country or an organization)" (Merriam-Webster, n.d.). For intermodal passenger facilities, governance typically involves multiple entities supported by strong partnerships. Effective governance and partnership agreements incorporate flexibility throughout the facility's life cycle and reflect the local stakeholder environment. Ineffective governance can contribute to project delays, cost overruns, legal disputes, and other negative impacts. Identifying the right governance model at project inception is an essential first step in project planning and sets the stage for positive outcomes.

Types of Governance Models

Different governance models are available for delivering, maintaining, and operating intermodal passenger facilities. The choice of model used often depends on local circumstances, types and scales of project delivery efficiencies, financing plans, and legal authority. The main types are:

- Single public entity,
- Public entity cooperative agreement,
- Public and joint powers authorities, and
- Special purpose vehicles and public–private partnerships.

Single Public Entity

When one entity owns an intermodal passenger facility and provides services directly or through vendors, its governance follows the entity's internal processes and procedures. The single entity can make all decisions and negotiate all agreements. In single public entity formats, partnerships tend to be internal. (See Coleman Dock example text box.)

Public Entity Cooperative Agreement

A public entity cooperative agreement involves two or more agencies that have distinct processes and procedures. Such agreements typically cover approaches to project funding/financing,

> **Single Public Entity: Coleman Dock**
>
> Washington State Ferries, a division of Washington DOT, began replacing the aging Seattle Coleman Dock in 2017 to enhance the ferry terminal's role as a regional multimodal transportation hub. Improvements include a new 1,900 passenger terminal, elevator access and other accessibility improvements, elevated pedestrian walkways, and an elevated connection across Alaskan Way via the Marion Street Walkway to/from Downtown Seattle.
>
> See the project website (https://wsdot.wa.gov/construction-planning/search-projects /ferries-seattle-multimodal-terminal-colman-dock-project) for more information.

delivery, and performance and may include identifying how roles and responsibilities are allocated and whose processes and procedures will govern the distinct phases of the asset's life cycle.

Public and Joint Powers Authorities

For more complex projects or programs that may involve multiple entities, governments often establish public authorities or joint powers authorities through legislation to develop and maintain public infrastructure. Such authorities may receive public funds, directly finance projects, and procure goods and services. Public authorities provide a single point of accountability and clear policies, processes, and procedures for making decisions throughout a project's life cycle. Public authorities also include procedures and policies to ensure transparency, accountability, and oversight, often reporting to a board made up of representatives of the partnering organizations. (See Greater Orlando Aviation Authority and Transbay Joint Powers Authority examples text box.)

Special Purpose Vehicle and Public–Private Partnerships

The U.S. DOT defines a public–private partnership (P3) as a contractual agreement formed between a public agency and a private entity that allows for greater private participation in transportation project delivery and financing (U.S. Department of Transportation 2024e). All P3s include financing, operations, and maintenance. See Appendix C for a more detailed discussion of using a P3 for delivering an intermodal passenger facility project.

> **Public–Private Partnership: LAX People Mover Station**
>
> The LAX People Mover connects the airport with a new Metro station, airport parking garages, and a new consolidated car rental facility. The project was developed under a P3 delivery model. Agreements among L.A. Metro and individual airlines delineated responsibilities for limits of the developer's work and those of other entities. The private developer is responsible for delivering and financing infrastructure, including the people mover system and its operations and maintenance. See the LAX automated people mover website (https://www.lawa.org/transforminglax/projects/underway/apm) for more information.

Public Authority: Greater Orlando Aviation Authority

The Greater Orlando Aviation Authority (GOAA) oversees airports in Orlando, Florida. As part of the new Orlando International Airport Terminal C expansion project, GOAA leased three platforms to Brightline, an intercity passenger rail line serving destinations in Florida. Brightline service opened at the airport in 2023. The terminal expansion project also includes a modern car rental facility with provisions for EV charging. See the Orlando International Airport press release website (https://www.orlandoairports.net/press/2022/09/13/orlando-internationals-new-terminal-c-arriving-on-schedule/) for more information.

Joint Powers Authority: Salesforce Transit Center

The Transbay Joint Powers Authority (TJPA) has primary jurisdiction for financing, design, development, construction, and operation of the Salesforce Transit Center (Transbay Terminal). Led by an eight-member board, TJPA was created by the City and County of San Francisco, the Alameda–Contra Costa Transit District, the Peninsula Corridor Joint Powers Board, the California High Speed Rail Authority, and Caltrans (ex officio).

See the About TJPA website (https://tjpa.org/tjpa/about-the-tjpa) for more information.

Essential Elements of the Governance Process

Regardless of the model chosen, successful governance of intermodal passenger facilities is built on a shared vision, identification of partners and stakeholders, and clearly defined stakeholder relationships.

Establishing a Shared Vision

Establishing a shared vision with potential partners and stakeholders is a critical first step in the planning and development process. *TCRP Report 102: Transit-Oriented Development in the United States: Experiences, Challenges, and Prospects* (Cervero et al. 2004) and *TCRP Report 224: Guide to Joint Development for Public Transportation Agencies* (Raine et al. 2021) provide examples of projects with shared visions.

As an example, for Arlington County, Virginia, maintaining a focus on its shared vision was critical to successful TOD implementation. Through a process that encompassed multiple stakeholders in the early 1970s, the county adopted a bull's eye metaphor to articulate its TOD goal (Cervero et al. 2004). This enabled the county to leverage Metrorail's presence and transform once dormant neighborhoods into vibrant clusters of office, retail, and residential development. The original vision and subsequent general plan and station area plans contributed to the realization of that vision. The county's ability to promote and sustain growth for over 40 years is the result of maintaining the original vision while adapting to the changing needs of its communities (Cervero et al. 2004).

Identifying Partners and Stakeholders

Strong coordination among partners and stakeholders is paramount to a successful intermodal passenger facility, particularly those that feature multiple modes of transportation and service providers. Each mode or service may have unique public or private stakeholders. Categorizing partners and stakeholders helps to clarify roles and responsibilities, which are then reflected in governance processes and procedures. Partners and stakeholders generally fall into three categories: direct participants, consulting parties, and external stakeholders.

Direct Participants

Direct participants include public entities with direct responsibility for the facility, and they typically include the property owner, a major tenant or operator, a major service provider, or public agencies with authority over the facility. Direct participants, either singly or jointly, have roles in governance and have ultimate decision-making authority. The direct participants' roles and responsibilities are codified through legal agreements, partnership agreements, contracts, or legislation.

Consulting Parties

Consulting parties may have a role in project delivery or facility management but are not involved with decision-making. Examples of consulting parties are public agencies with review or permitting roles, project abutters, public safety agencies, contractors, project tenants, and modal operating agencies. Agreements with consulting parties may take the form of contracts, cooperative agreements, interface agreements, memorandums of understanding, and operating agreements. These flow from the authority of the direct participants.

External Stakeholders

External stakeholders are public and private entities with an outside interest in an intermodal passenger facility. External stakeholders include community organizations, neighborhood or business associations, and advocates. Intermodal passenger facility projects need well-established plans for external stakeholder communication. Appointed project advisory committees are often used for this purpose. In some instances, specific communication protocols can be established between the primary participants and the external stakeholders to outline the types and schedules of communication.

Defining Stakeholder Relationships

The process of defining stakeholder relationships typically begins with mapping all facility stakeholders and grouping them into functional categories, such as owners, customers, transportation providers, service providers, and community groups. Figure 8 illustrates a mapping example for airport stakeholders that is derived from the International Air Transport Association (IATA) Airport Governance Toolkit (Reece and Robinson 2020). This comprehensive example helps to illustrate parties directly involved in an airport (e.g., facility owner, airlines, owners), consulting parties (e.g., government and related entities), and external entities (e.g., communities). The mapping process in this example also considers other important stakeholders, such as consumers and passengers, modal providers (airlines and surface transportation providers), and retail tenants.

Assigning Roles and Responsibilities

Because intermodal passenger facility projects often involve several public and private entities as well as external stakeholders, project planners should address certain key questions while defining relationships, roles, and responsibilities, including:

- Who has the legal authority to participate in the project? Is a legislative change required to include the pertinent parties?

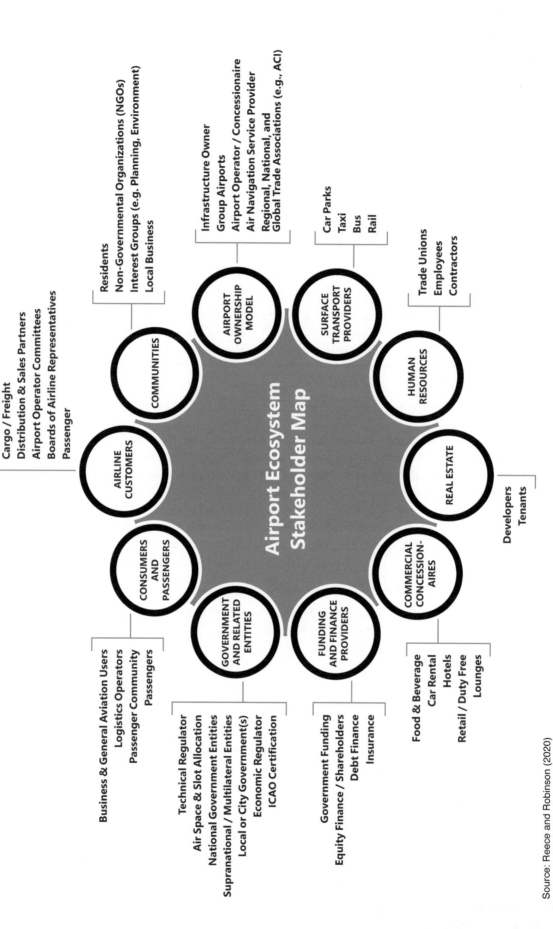

Source: Reece and Robinson (2020)

Figure 8. Example stakeholder map.

- Who can provide funding for the project? Is financing available and by whom? Can equity/revenue flow to the project and, if so, through what party?
- Who has property rights, including land ownership, leases, and development rights?
- Whose regulations and standards will apply and who has oversight?
- Who will sustain and maintain the project through its life cycle?
- Who has responsibility for safety and security?

For governance purposes, entities identified through this initial set of questions are then typically divided into direct participants, consulting participants, and external stakeholders.

Using a RACI Matrix to Assign Roles and Responsibilities

RACI (responsible, accountable, consulted, informed) is an acronym for a type of responsibility matrix specifying who is responsible for a task, who is accountable for a task, who needs to be consulted, and who needs to be informed. A RACI matrix is helpful when projects have multiple participating entities performing different tasks that feature multiple timelines, key milestones, and decision points. RACI is commonly used for managing different types of construction, implementation, and monitoring activities (AASHTO 2024).

A RACI matrix or other matrix approach can help inform the structuring of governance agreements. Once roles and responsibilities are established, legal agreements, contracts, and legislation can be developed to formally establish the relationships among the parties. Figure 9 presents an example for a hypothetical intermodal passenger facility.

PROCESS	Planning		Design		Construction		Occupancy
ROLE OF PARTIES	Delivery	Financing	Communications	Ownership	Operations	Maintenance	Decision-Making
Facility Owner	R	C	R	R	C	C	R
Modal Provider 1			C	C	A	A	C
Modal Provider 2			C	C	A	A	C
Government Agency 1		R	C				R
Government Agency 2		C	C				R
Lead Developer	A	A	C	R	R	R	C
Permitting Authority	C	I	I				R
Community Association	I		I		I		I

R Responsible **A** Accountable **C** Consulted **I** Informed

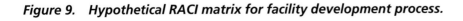

Figure 9.   Hypothetical RACI matrix for facility development process.

Accommodating Changes Over a Project's Life Cycle

Stakeholder roles and responsibilities may evolve as a project moves from inception to delivery to operations and maintenance. Governance models should take into consideration the full life cycle and what roles each party may play at different times. Flexible governance agreements consider the different roles parties may play during planning, design, construction, and operations and maintenance phases of the project. In addition, the governance model should be flexible and designed to accommodate potential changes in roles and responsibilities.

Governance Model Checklist

A governance model should address all aspects of the intermodal passenger facility, from planning and delivery through operations and maintenance. Once a model that clarifies roles and responsibilities is created, governance agreements can be created. Regardless of the model of governance, all governance agreements should include these elements:

- A statement of the shared vision for the project and its objectives.
- An outline of the relationships between all internal and external partners and stakeholders and those with property interests.
- A formal agreement among the direct participants that identifies a structure with a single point of authority for decision-making.
- Authority for representing the project in contracting and working with external stakeholders and third parties throughout its life cycle.
- A preliminary financing plan that identifies sources and uses of funds, conditions for receiving grant funds or revenues, and potential for creating incentives to foster cooperative behavior. (See Chapter 8.)
- Considerations for future expansion.
- An agreement on management mechanisms for:
  - Processes and procedures,
  - Independent reviews and oversight,
  - Dispute resolution,
  - Approving changes, and
  - Reporting and transparency.

Documenting the approaches to these governance framework essentials and identifying the strategies to implement them will contribute to successful project delivery and high levels of performance throughout the facility's useful life. Spending time early in the intermodal passenger facility development process to document the approach to governance and implementing the framework is a critical first step in project development.

Flexible Governance at Denver Union Station

The Denver Union project illustrates how governance can change over time. The City of Denver originally adopted the Denver Union Station Master Plan in 2004. Four years later, the Denver Union Station Project Authority (DUSPA), a nonprofit, public benefit corporation was established to finance and oversee project implementation. Partners included Regional Transportation District (RTD), the City and County of Denver, Colorado DOT, and the Denver Regional Council of Governments. Since project completion, RTD is responsible for station elements while a private developer is responsible for the historic station building. (See Appendix D.)

Project Delivery Methods

With a governance model in place and project planning and permitting complete (scoping, environmental evaluation and clearance, property acquisition, initial business case and financial plan), the next step is to select a method of project delivery. The following discussion offers a high-level summary of available methods. Appendix C provides more details on project delivery methods, including on structures and timelines.

Design–Bid–Build

Design–bid–build (DBB) is a common method of project delivery that many government entities use. Each project phase (design and construction) is bid out sequentially through separate procurements. The public owner or project sponsor manages the interfaces between the designer and contractor. The designer develops the design and specifications to a level near 100%, and the owner uses a procurement process for the construction components. The construction contracts are bid based on 100% design drawings and specifications. In a DBB procurement, the owner assumes risks for cost and schedule.

Construction Management/General Contractor

Construction management/general contractor (CM/GC) is a progressive project delivery option. A CM/GC is delivered in two phases (preconstruction and construction). This method is also known as construction manager at risk (CMAR). This delivery method brings the contractor on at the 30% level of design and requires delivery at a guaranteed maximum price.

Design–Build

Design–build (DB) integrates different elements of delivery into a single contract. Project owners typically develop concept designs to approximately 30% and then initiate a procurement process to engage a contractor with design experience or a team that includes contractors and designers. The procurement process itself can be interactive by allowing bidding teams to propose alternative technical concepts and innovative solutions to reduce costs and accelerate the schedule.

As with CMAR, this delivery method brings the contractor on early at a 30% level of design and transfers design and construction integration from the owner to the contractor. However, the level of design requires contractors to take a larger share of risk on unknowns because of the limited design stage. This can lead to more claims and changes for the owner if unknowns are encountered.

Progressive Design–Build

Progressive design–build (PDB) is gaining in popularity. Like CM/GC, under a PDB framework, the owner chooses a designer/builder based on qualifications. The relationship between parties is like that with a DB contract in that the designer is working for the contractor instead of the owner; however, PDB includes two distinct phases: development and delivery.

A PDB delivery approach provides greater flexibility than a DB approach by defining and de-risking the project during the development phase. Once the project scope is defined to a sufficient detail, the PDB contractor then submits a hard bid for the delivery phase, which is negotiated with the owner on an open-book basis.

The development phase fosters an opportunity for the contractor to partner with the owner to further progress the design, determine the need for early work packages, and arrive at a more confident project cost. This method can reduce the overall delivery schedule and potential claims but has the disadvantage of the owner negotiating with a single party.

Design–Build–Operate–Maintain

In most intermodal passenger facility projects, the owner is ultimately responsible for facility operations and maintenance and receives the facility back from the contractor once construction is complete. Under a design–build–operate–maintain (DBOM) delivery model, the same team involved with DB or PDB is also responsible for operations and maintenance over a defined period. DBOM projects typically require the contractor to meet performance measures during the operations and maintenance period to ensure that the facility is well maintained throughout the term. With DBOM, the overall project design and selection of construction materials place greater emphasis on durability of materials to optimize life-cycle costs since the DBOM contractor is concerned with the whole life of the asset. DBOM contracts typically include risk-sharing provisions and incentives to encourage cooperation between the contractor and the owner.

Public–Private Partnerships

P3s combine design, construction, financing, and operations and maintenance under one contract. P3s are performance-based contracts. They are often used when an owner wants to accelerate delivery of a facility and combine that with performance-based operations and maintenance over a set term. It is important to have a defined project scope, environmental clearance, performance-based specifications, and a project champion representing the owner.

P3s require expertise from public owners that they may not have in-house. Because P3s are complex, public owners should have competent legal, financial, and technical advisers in place to assist with development of procurement documents and throughout the procurement process. It can take more than 2 years to procure and negotiate a P3 contract, but the benefits of an integrated delivery with project financing and a performance-based operations and maintenance contract can overcome the disadvantages of a lengthy procurement time frame.

Evaluating Project Delivery Models

When evaluating project delivery options, project planners and owners should determine the legal authorities available, the goals for the procurement, and how each option meets the goals, which can include cost and schedule certainty, speed of delivery, integration of services, degree of risk transfer, and compatibility with existing services available to the owner. The evaluation process is typically both qualitative and quantitative.

Qualitative Comparison of Project Delivery

A qualitative comparison can identify necessary trade-offs to achieve stakeholder consensus. For more complex intermodal passenger facility projects, more than one delivery model may be appropriate for different project elements. For example, the redevelopment of Denver Union Station and the surrounding TOD project used a P3 for the station while a private real estate development team redeveloped the project around the station.

As an example, see Figure 10, which shows, by goal category, a hypothetical evaluation using the six models discussed in this chapter. In this example, the project goal was to quickly deliver a facility funded through facility revenue and downstream grants. The qualitative analysis indicated that P3 would be the most promising delivery model. P3 works in this instance because

GOALS / DELIVERY METHOD	DESIGN-BID-BUILD	CM/GC	DESIGN-BUILD	PROGRESSIVE DESIGN-BUILD	DBOM	PUBLIC-PRIVATE PARTNERSHIP (P3)
Meet aggressive schedule	○	◑	◕	●	◕	●
Provide early cost certainty	○	◔	●	◕	●	◕
Minimize risk of cost overruns	◕	◕	◑	◕	◑	◕
Maximize stakeholder collaboration	●	◕	◑	◑	◕	◕
Allow phased funding	◑	●	○	●	○	●
Maximize competition among bidders	●	○	●	○	●	○
Allow contractor involvement/innovation	○	●	◕	●	◕	●
Maximize partnership opportunities	○	●	◑	●	◑	●
Limit changes between design and construction	○	◑	●	◕	●	●
Integrate operations & maintenance	○	○	○	○	●	●

Most favorable > ● ◕ ◑ ◔ ○ < Least favorable

Source: WSP

Figure 10. Hypothetical qualitative comparison of project delivery methods.

of the project's accelerated schedule; the ability to meet the funding profile; the integration of design, construction, and operations and maintenance; the ability to enhance innovation; and price and schedule certainty. A PDB delivery option also scores well but does not include operations and maintenance services.

Quantitative Analysis of Project Delivery Options

Following the qualitative evaluation, a quantitative analysis can be used for the most promising options to evaluate specific project risk assessments, update cost estimates, and compare schedules and conceptual financing plans for each delivery model. It is important that the analysis receive input from identified stakeholders and that they understand their roles, responsibilities, and how each delivery model will affect their workstreams and overall project governance. Table 9 shows the overall approach (both qualitative and quantitative analysis) to the selection of a delivery method.

Private Development Partnerships

Many intermodal passenger facilities include a private development component, either within the facility or adjacent to it. Assuming market conditions support a mix of new land uses to complement the facility, there are a variety of ways to integrate development. In most cases, this

Table 9.   Qualitative and quantitative analysis of project delivery methods.

Qualitative Analysis		Quantitative Analysis	
Options	Constraints	Feasibility study	Preferred option
Procurement method	Stakeholder objectives	Refinement of cost and revenue estimates	Variation over phases
Project scope	Market appetite	Risk analysis	Risk allocation
Phasing	Potential public funds	Financial structure	Governance
	Legal	Value of options comparison	Legal changes
	Regulatory		Range of funding need

Source: WSP

future development potential can and should be factored into the overall governance model and used as a source of potential funding. Ultimately, the most appropriate land development model will depend on who has property rights, including ownership and control of the developable area under consideration.

Joint Development

Depending on the development scenario and owner goals, developable land can be sold outright or developed through ground or air-rights leases. Detailed guidance on a range of development options is provided in *TCRP Research Report 224: Guide to Joint Development for Public Transit Agencies* (Raine et al. 2021). This report describes best practices for public transit agencies to optimize joint development opportunities and provides detailed guidance on each step of the process. The report defines joint development by its transactional relationship to the transit agency and its ability to generate lease or sale proceeds, cost avoidance arrangements, or other forms of financial return.

The scale and mix of potential uses will also influence the land development model and eventual selection of a single developer partner, multiple partners, or a master developer. In a scenario where there is a limited inventory of developable land, a single developer partner may be selected to deliver a specific use on a parcel or parcels. If the scale of developable land availability and development potential is larger, a master developer land development model may be more applicable. In this scenario, the master developer typically acquires the land and oversees the phased development of several parcels and uses. This model ensures that there is a holistic approach to the timing, scale, and mix of uses and that there is a cohesive planning framework around the intermodal passenger facility.

Provider Partnerships

Intermodal passenger facility owners may choose to form partnerships with modal providers and with others local entities. These include transportation management associations (TMAs), private mobility providers, social service agencies, and community-based organizations.

Transportation Management Associations

TMAs are nonprofit organizations made up of various public and private stakeholders collaborating to address specific transportation issues. TMAs often focus on alternatives to driving alone. While TMA funding traditionally derives from employed membership, federal grants in partnership with local jurisdictions have become more common in recent years. [The Association for Commuter Transportation (https://www.actweb.org/) is a valuable resource for working with TMAs.]

Shared Mobility Providers

Cities across the United States (and the world) have responded to the growth in private shared mobility companies operating bikesharing, scooter sharing, ridehailing, and other services by requiring companies to obtain operating permits. Contracts with local governments typically include per-vehicle deployment fees and annual application renewal fees. In exchange, cities often limit the number of shared mobility providers allowed to enter the market, sometimes granting exclusive rights to operate within the market. Fees from these agreements can then be earmarked for infrastructure improvements, maintenance, or expansion.

TCRP Research Report 204: Partnerships Between Transit Agencies and Transportation Network Companies (TNCs) provides a review of partnerships between transit agencies and TNCs in the United States. (Curtis et al. 2019). The report also presents a partnership playbook that offers step-by-step guidance to transit practitioners interested in pursuing partnerships with TNCs. *TCRP Research Report 221: Redesigning Transit Networks for the New Mobility Future* (Byala et al. 2021) includes toolkits for leveraging partnerships with other entities and for working with the private sector.

Intermodal passenger facilities can also work with the local government to impose a small surcharge for each ridehailing/TNC trip. Trips to and from airports or major train stations could have additional surcharges for construction and maintenance of accommodating facilities.

Moreover, bikeshare programs such as Citi Bike in New York City and Divvy in Chicago have emerged through public–private partnerships. These partnerships unlock private investment through additional funding opportunities such as advertising revenue and corporate sponsorships. Also see the micromobility discussion in Chapter 6.

CHAPTER 8

Funding and Financing

Introduction

Intermodal passenger facility projects are often costly and complex undertakings requiring substantial financial resources. Project owners typically work with multiple entities to explore all possible sources of funding, financing options, and partnerships to complete and maintain facility projects.

This chapter discusses ways to choose the right funding program and financing approach and summarizes the funding, financing, and innovative delivery options available. Appendix D provides detailed information on funding sources available as of this report's publication. Appendix E is a case study of Denver Union Station's innovative financing and project delivery approach.

For the purposes of this report, funding is considered to be any resource available directly from federal, state, or local public entities to pay for an intermodal passenger facility's up-front capital costs and ongoing operating costs, including funds that may be required to pay debt service. Financing represents borrowing (and other strategies) to pay for project capital costs over time.

Choosing the Right Funding Program/Approach

The process of choosing among funding programs and financing approaches is illustrated in Figure 11 and includes the following elements, each described further in this chapter.

- Conducting the initial project assessment.
- Establishing the base financial condition.
- Identifying new funding and financing requirements.
- Preparing the grant application.

Conduct Initial Project Assessment

Intermodal facility project owners should initially assess the project scope, completion schedule, and costs for constructing, operating, and maintaining the facility. This step also includes determining whether the project will produce revenue and identifying potential risks.

Establish Base Financial Condition

Once an intermodal passenger facility owner understands the associated costs and risks, the next step for the owner is to know the project's baseline financial condition, including the

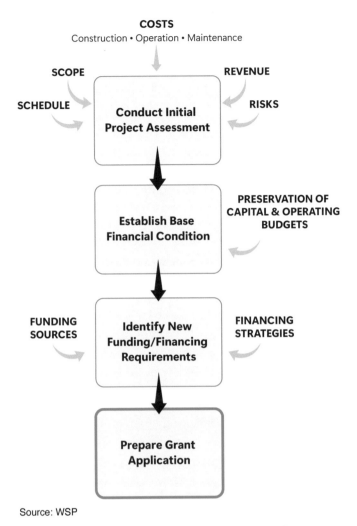

Source: WSP

***Figure 11.   Funding and financing approach
flowchart.***

potential use of existing funding. This analysis must take into consideration how much existing funding can be used without harming the entity's future financial outlook, capital improvement plans, and operating budgets. The amount of the project that the owner cannot fund is the funding gap.

Identify New Funding and Financing Requirements

Owners are advised to consider all available federal funding and innovative financing opportunities that are available and most align with the project's needs. When considering grant funding opportunities, applicants should note the minimum and maximum award requirements, whether there is a required match, and what type of project activities are allowed. For financing opportunities, owners should consider the terms of the agreement, including the interest rate, the principal available, and the length of repayment. The owner can then prioritize opportunities based on what aligns best with the project.

Understand Prior Funding Restrictions

Owners of existing facilities are advised to consult funding agreements when renovating a facility constructed with government funds.

Prepare the Grant Application

For each prioritized grant program, owners should develop a timeline for the application development. Owners are encouraged to review prior notices of funding opportunities (NOFOs), including timing of notices and decisions to establish expected time frames for application and award. The timeline should list potential grant programs and their expected timing. In addition, owners should review the NOFOs to identify elements that will make the project's story compelling, and should use data and analysis to convey the story. Most grants are awarded to projects that are close to being shovel ready, so advancing design, securing environmental clearances, obtaining required permits, and documenting local funding commitments and regional support will all help to make a more compelling and competitive case for a grant award.

Federal Funding Strategies

There are numerous federal funding and financing strategies applicable to the development of new and expanded/renovated intermodal passenger facilities. The following discussion describes funding sources and financing options as of this report's publication. Most of the funding is authorized through federal fiscal year (FFY) 2026. Reauthorization or new legislation is needed to continue these programs. Several of the funding programs have been in effect for decades and can be expected to be continued.

While financing intermodal passenger facility projects can help pay for up-front capital costs, this approach typically costs more in terms of future debt serviced on the borrowed funds. Financing also typically requires a dedicated local repayment source. The passage of the Bipartisan Infrastructure Law also made financing programs more attractive and accessible for local municipalities.

Federal funding programs include discretionary grant opportunities and formula programs administered by U.S. DOT and its modal administrations, including FHWA, FTA, FRA, the Maritime Administration, and FAA. General formula and grant programs apply to the following four categories of funding:

- Multimodal transportation projects,
- Vehicle funding programs,
- Roadway funding programs, and
- Funding for airports, marine ports, and railroads.

Many of the federal funding programs provide resources for multiple types of capital expenditures, including for vehicles and facilities. Appendix D describes each program and includes detailed tables of matching requirements, eligibility, funding amounts through FY 2026, and typical award size. Readers are also encouraged to consult the U.S. DOT website (https://www.transportation.gov/grants) for current information on grant programs.

General Formula and Grant Programs

General formula and grant programs provide funding for a range of multimodal transportation projects and provide the greatest range of eligible activities. (See Table 10.) Seven of these nine general programs can be used to fund planning, design, or construction. The general programs are split between four formula programs and five discretionary grant programs.

Federal Vehicle Funding Programs

The vehicle funding programs provide formula and discretionary grant funds for transit vehicle acquisition, including ZEV fleets, supporting facilities such as EV charging infrastructure, and ferries. (See Table 11.)

Table 10.   Federal general formulas and grants.

Program	Type
FHWA Carbon Reduction Program	Formula
FHWA Congestion Mitigation and Air Quality Improvement (CMAQ)	Formula
FHWA Surface Transportation	Formula
FTA Sections 5303, 5304, and 5305	Formula
FTA Transit-Oriented Development (TOD) Planning Program	Grant
U.S. DOT National Infrastructure Project Assistance (MEGA)	Grant
U.S. DOT Rebuilding American Infrastructure with Sustainability and Equity (RAISE)	Grant
U.S. DOT Rural Surface Transportation	Grant
U.S. DOT Strengthening Mobility and Revolutionizing Transportation (SMART)	Grant

See Appendix D for matching requirements, eligibility, current funding amounts, and typical award size.

Table 11.   Federal vehicle funding programs.

Program	Type
FHWA Charging and Fueling Infrastructure (CFI) Discretionary Grant Program	Grant
FHWA National Electric Vehicle Infrastructure (NEVI) Formula Program	Formula
FTA Ferry Programs	Grant
FTA Section 5339 (a), (b), and (c)	Formula/grant

See Appendix D for matching requirements, eligibility, current funding amounts, and typical award size.

Federal Roadway Funding Programs

Roadway programs support the development of bicycle, pedestrian, and road infrastructure and can be used to support such infrastructure at intermodal passenger facilities. (See Table 12.)

Federal Funding for Rail, Aviation, Maritime, and Transit Stations

Table 13 shows funding options for passenger rail, rail infrastructure and safety, airports, ports, and rail stations.

Financing Options and Innovative Delivery Strategies

Ideally, maximizing funding from the many sources described in this chapter would cover the entire public cost of delivering a project. If there is a funding gap after all possible public funding sources have been exhausted, the remaining capital cost shortfall is generally assumed

Table 12.   Federal roadway funding programs.

Program	Type
FHWA Advanced Transportation Technologies and Innovation (ATTAIN) Program	Grant
FHWA Highway Safety Improvement Program (HSIP)	Formula
U.S. DOT Nationally Significant Multimodal Freight and Highway (INFRA) Program	Grant
U.S. DOT Neighborhood Access and Equity (NAE) Grant Program	Grant
U.S. DOT Reconnecting Communities Pilot Program	Grant
U.S. DOT Safe Streets and Roads for All (SS4A) Grant Program	Grant

See Appendix D for matching requirements, eligibility, current funding amounts, and typical award size.

Table 13. **Federal funding for airports, ports, and railroads.**

Program	Type
FAA Airport Improvement Program (AIP)	Formula/grant
FAA Airport Terminal Program (ATP)	Grant
FAA Passenger Facility Charge (PFC) Local User Fee	Fee
FRA Consolidated Rail Infrastructure and Safety Improvements (CRISI) Program	Grant
FRA Federal-State Partnership for Intercity Passenger Rail Grant Program	Grant
FTA All Stations Accessibility Program (ASAP)	Grant
U.S. DOT Port Infrastructure Development Program (PIDP)	Grant

See Appendix D for matching requirements, eligibility, current funding amounts, and typical award size.

to be covered by some form of public financing or an alternative revenue source. If a funding gap is large, and available debt financing terms are less favorable or flexible, future revenue streams from the project may not be sufficient to cover the resulting debt, and the project will not be financially feasible. Maximizing funding from all possible federal, state, and local sources can minimize the funding shortfall and the resulting debt issuance required.

The following section describes some common debt financing mechanisms available at the federal level (and state/local level, depending on the location) as well as innovative, project-specific mechanisms that may be available for consideration for intermodal passenger facilities.

For intermodal passenger facility projects, these additional, project-specific mechanisms generally leverage two primary opportunities that these projects tend to catalyze: (1) land use/future development potential, and (2) mobility-focused revenue-generation potential. In each case, successfully generating revenue from land use and mobility opportunities requires significant planning and time to develop and structure partnerships with the necessary public- and private-sector stakeholders. Such opportunities also have implications for the types of governance structures that may be most applicable, depending on the given scenario.

Federal Financing Options

The two main federal financing options for intermodal passenger facility projects are commonly known as TIFIA and RRIF (see the following two subsections).

Transportation Infrastructure Finance and Innovation Act and TIFIA 49

The Transportation Infrastructure Finance and Innovation Act (TIFIA) provides low-cost financing to fill funding gaps in infrastructure projects. TIFIA credit assistance is available as direct loans, loan guarantees, and standby lines of credit to finance surface transportation projects of national and regional significance (U.S. Department of Transportation 2024a). Credit assistance has historically been capped at 33% of reasonably anticipated eligible project costs. However, in 2022, the U.S. DOT introduced the TIFIA 49 initiative, which increased the maximum loan amount from 33% to 49% of project costs for eligible transit and TOD projects. In addition to this increase, the IIJA has made TIFIA credit assistance more attainable and flexible by (1) relaxing requirements for investment-grade ratings, and (2) increasing the maximum loan duration from 35 years to 75 years for projects with an estimated life greater than 50 years (U.S. Department of Transportation 2024a).

TIFIA loan eligibility was also expanded to include port, TOD, and airport terminal and airside projects. To be eligible, these types of projects must be added to State Transportation Improvement Program (STIP) project lists under special exceptions (U.S. Department of Transportation 2024a).

> ### Miami Intermodal Center Use of TIFIA
>
> Miami Intermodal Center blended multiple federal, state, and local funding sources to fund a $2 billion project to improve ground travel to and within Miami International Airport. As part of these sources, the project secured a $270 million loan from TIFIA and $6 million in federal grants. See https://www.fhwa.dot.gov /ipd/project_profiles/fl_miami_intermodal.aspx for more information.

Railroad Rehabilitation and Improvement Financing

The Railroad Rehabilitation and Improvement Financing (RRIF) program provides federal credit assistance in the form of direct loans, loan guarantees, and lines of credit to finance rail projects. RRIF offers direct loans for up to 100% of the project cost (or up to 75% for eligible TOD projects). The program allows a repayment period of up to 75 years after the date of substantial completion of the project, pursuant to the IIJA. The RRIF program is authorized to provide up to $35 billion in direct loans and loan guarantees to finance development of railroad infrastructure, with $7 billion reserved for freight railroads other than Class I carriers (railroads with operating revenue of less than $272.0 million annually). In addition, the IIJA, subject to appropriations, added discretionary credit assistance of $50 million per year up to $20 million per loan. At least 50% of such credit assistance is set aside for freight railroads other than Class I carriers. Furthermore, the IIJA made TOD a permanent project eligibility. Lastly, the infrastructure law codified the RRIF express program, which establishes an expedited credit review process for loans that meet certain financial and operational criteria and requires regular updates from U.S. DOT on status of application so as to reduce applicant uncertainty (U.S. Department of Transportation 2024a).

Eligible applicants for RRIF financing include railroads, state and local governments, government-sponsored authorities and corporations, limited-option freight shippers that intend to construct a new rail connection, and joint ventures that include at least one of the preceding categories. The FRA notes that RRIF financing may be used to:

- Acquire, improve, or rehabilitate intermodal or rail equipment or facilities, including track, components of track, bridges, yards, buildings and shops, and the installation of positive train control systems;
- Develop or establish new intermodal or railroad facilities;
- Reimburse planning and design expenses relating to these activities;
- Refinance outstanding debt incurred for the purposes listed previously; and
- Finance TOD (U.S. Department of Transportation 2024a).

Other Financing Options

Additional intermodal passenger facility financing options include:

- User fees,
- Dedicated taxes,

- Tax-exempt municipal bonds,
- State infrastructure bank loans,
- Private activity bonds,
- P3 financing, and
- Value capture (U.S. Department of Transportation 2024a).

User Fees

User fees are a common funding source for financing construction, operations, and maintenance. Bonds backed by future user fee revenues help fund capital costs. The fees can be direct (facility users) or indirect tolls or fees. Entities implementing user fees must decide how to collect them and when to adjust rates in the future. One risk from this method is that it can be difficult to raise future rates to keep up with increasing maintenance costs (Dornan and March 2005).

Dedicated Taxes

Dedicated taxes can be levied to support intermodal passenger facility construction, operations, and maintenance. As with user fees, bonds can be issued backed by future tax revenues. Dedicated taxes may be local or state taxes, usage taxes (e.g., for rental cars or lodging), or license-based taxes such as on ridehailing companies. Enacting taxes or fees to support an intermodal passenger facility project is often a potentially lengthy and politically challenging process.

Tax-Exempt Municipal Bonds

Tax-exempt municipal bonds are the most common debt instrument used by state or local governments to finance infrastructure projects. Government agencies and eligible nonprofit entities may directly issue bonds that are exempt from federal taxes, which reduces interest rates and financing costs. Issuers are also often exempt from state and local taxes, further reducing interest rates and financing costs. Laws in some states permit both state and local funding partners to use tax-exempt bonds to fund the state and local share of project costs. In other states, limitations on bonding capacity or insufficient revenues preclude this option.

State Infrastructure Bank Loans

State infrastructure bank (SIB) loans are revolving loan programs funded with seed money from the federal or state government. SIB programs provide loans or loan guarantees that are repaid with project revenues or pledged funding from state or local sources. The repayment terms are often very flexible, often allowing for deferral of principal payments. Program availability and specific loan terms vary by state but, if available, can be a complementary source of financing combined with other sources such as TIFIA loans.

Private Activity Bonds

Private activity bonds (PABs) are tax-exempt securities issued by public entities to finance privately developed infrastructure that benefits the public. PABs offer lower financing costs when compared to taxable debt. The private sector is responsible for paying the PABs back and assumes all financial risk. PABs require private-sector interest and a public entity to serve as a conduit. Like SIB loans, program availability, debt issuance terms, and project eligibility can vary by state. At the federal level, PAB eligibility automatically includes any project that is eligible for TIFIA credit assistance, which includes multimodal facilities (U.S. Department of Transportation 2024a).

P3 Financing

The two most typical types of P3 financing are P3 equity and P3 debt. P3 equity represents a private ownership stake in an enterprise with an aim of making a profitable return and may include investment from commercial developers, financial investors, pension funds, sovereign wealth funds, insurance companies, and private equity funds. A P3 equity stake is just one component of an overall project delivery strategy. P3 debt can be coupled with equity to finance the initial investment and may include PABs, taxable bonds, bank loans, and other debt instruments. P3s have the potential to support a significant share of project costs and could facilitate lower project costs as part of a comprehensive program delivery strategy. However, the resulting transfer of project risk to the private sector typically requires that program sponsors also transfer some direct control of the program (U.S. Department of Transportation 2024a).

Value Capture

P3 and TIFIA Financing: Salesforce Transit Center

Salesforce Transit Center in San Francisco, CA, relied on local, regional, state, federal, and private funding to assist with the funding of the project. This included a $171 million TIFIA loan and over $400 million in federal grant funds, and a $154 million bridge loan from a private entity. See https://www.fhwa.dot.gov/ipd/project_profiles/ca_transbay_transit.aspx for more information.

Value capture is the concept of capturing the enhanced real estate value attributable to a public improvement (such as transit or other TOD-supportive infrastructure) to help fund that improvement. Value capture can be categorized as joint development and a family of methods known as district value capture, which includes tax increment financing and special assessment districts (Raine et al. 2021).

Joint Development

Depending on the type of real estate transaction structure involved, the public revenue from joint development can be generated in a variety of ways. In cases where the public landowner wishes to maintain ownership of the property in the future, it can participate in the development as a partner, collecting an agreed upon share of future development revenue. Other transactions that require less ongoing involvement by the public entity include long-term ground leases and long-term air-rights leases. The terms of such leases can be negotiated to include a steady stream of annual payments; a large, one-time, up-front payment; or some combination depending on what works best for all parties involved. Other models include collecting proceeds from the outright sale of excess land and from collecting rents of on-site space from commercial tenants. *TCRP Report 224: Guide to Joint Development for Public Transportation Agencies* (Raine et al. 2021) provides extensive information on this topic.

District Value Capture

Tax Increment Financing

In general terms, tax increment financing (TIF) is a mechanism for capturing all or part of the increased property tax paid by properties within a designated area. TIF is not an additional tax, nor does it deprive governments of existing property tax revenues up to a set base within the TIF district. Instead, part of or all future property taxes (above the set base level) resulting from increased property values or from new development are dedicated to paying for the public improvement that caused the value increases and additional development (Federal Highway Administration Center for Innovative Finance Support, n.d.-a).

Special Assessment Districts

Special tax assessments are additional taxes paid within defined geographic areas or districts where landowners receive a direct and unique benefit from a public improvement. Generally, the cost of the improvement is allocated to property owners within the defined benefit zone and collected in conjunction with property or sales taxes over a predetermined number of years. The assessment is eliminated once the annual assessment collections cover the cost of the improvement (or debt issued to pay for the improvement) (Federal Highway Administration Center for Innovative Finance Support, n.d.-a).

Development Impact Fees

Development impact fees and excise taxes are one-time charges collected from developers or property owners to fund public infrastructure and services made necessary by new development. Impact fees are most successfully implemented in areas poised for significant growth with little or no existing development. Generally, rates are based on a formula that takes into consideration the number of new dwelling units or square feet of nonresidential space and the relative benefit the infrastructure provides the property. For transportation projects, relative benefit is usually determined by a development's distance from the improvement (Federal Highway Administration Center for Innovative Finance Support, n.d.-a).

CHAPTER 9

Conclusion

Each intermodal passenger facility is unique. The planning and decision-making process should reflect the facility's uniqueness as well as its relationship to the local context, its surrounding environment, and the broader community. At the same time, the intermodal passenger facility's main function is to serve people undertaking a journey. By prioritizing the experience of the customer (regardless of income, ability, or spoken language), planners, owners, and providers can better adapt to changing trends and make informed decisions. Efforts to advance the complete trip concept, expand MaaS to include all modes of transportation, emphasize effective governance, broaden partnerships, and better manage facility pickup and drop-off can all lead to improved facility operations and an enhanced user experience.

Key Takeaways

The following are additional key takeaways from the research effort that are intended to serve as high-level themes and for future consideration.

Collaborate Early and Often

Intermodal passenger facility planners, owners, and modal providers need to regularly collaborate with each other and with external stakeholders. This ongoing need begins with governance and continues with partnerships. Owners, providers, and other partners should always be considering the customer's travel experience traveling to, within, and from the entire facility instead of just considering the customer as using only one mode of travel. Collaboration also includes forming and maintaining strong partnerships with external stakeholders to address non-transportation matters that can affect a facility, such as coordinating responses to extreme weather events or working to address the housing crisis.

Identify Ways to Streamline Intermodal Passenger Facility Projects

Intermodal passenger facility projects take many years to implement. As projects advance, construction costs continue to escalate, changes to the climate may accelerate, and plans developed today may be obsolete at project completion. More research may be needed on streamlining intermodal passenger facility projects to ensure that they address current needs and are affordable.

Plan with Flexibility in Mind and Adapt Accordingly

Even with shorter implementation time frames, intermodal travel will continue to evolve and emerging technologies will continue to change travel behavior. Planning with flexibility and adaptability means assuming that decisions made today will need to be revised in the future. This means working to avoid being constrained by decisions that will be hard to reverse.

Collect Data More Often and Share It More Broadly

Facility owners and modal providers need to regularly collect data that measure usage patterns and then use these data to improve facility operations and the user experience. This means regularly conducting passenger surveys, measuring how people enter and exit a facility, investing in automated systems to collect data, and sharing the data, including through open sources and in ways that are agnostic to the individual mode or the technology used.

References

Airports Worldwide. n.d. Kansas City International Airport. https://www.airports-worldwide.com/usa/missouri/kansas_city_international_missouri.php.

AASHTO. 2024. AASHTO Transportation Asset Management Guide. https://www.tamguide.com/.

Amtrak. n.d. Historic Timeline. https://history.amtrak.com/amtraks-history/historic-timeline.

APTA. 2011. Why Design Matters for Transit. https://www.apta.com/wp-content/uploads/Standards_Documents/APTA-SUDS-UD-RP-003-11.pdf.

APTA. 2013. Best Practices for Integrating Art into Capital Projects. APTA, Washington, DC. https://www.apta.com/wp-content/uploads/Standards_Documents/APTA-SUDS-UD-RP-007-13_Booklet_Version.pdf.

APTA. 2021. 2021 *Public Transportation Fact Book*.

Argonne National Laboratory. n.d. Light Duty Electric Drive Vehicles Monthly Sales Updates. https://www.anl.gov/esia/light-duty-electric-drive-vehicles-monthly-sales-updates.

Badger E. and E. Washington. 2022. The Housing Shortage Isn't Just a Coastal Crisis Anymore. https://www.nytimes.com/2022/07/14/upshot/housing-shortage-us.html.

Byala, L., S. Johnson, R. Slocum, A. Zalewski, J. Weiland, L. Culp, B. Eby, P. Lewis, G. Calves, and D. Sampson. 2021. *TCRP Research Report 221: Redesigning Transit Networks for the New Mobility Future*. Transportation Research Board, Washington, DC. https://doi.org/10.17226/26028.

Boudreau, B., G. Detmer, S. Box, R. Burke, J. Paternoster, and L. Carbone. 2016. *ACRP Report 157: Improving the Airport Customer Experience*. National Academies Press, Washington, DC. https://doi.org/10.17226/23449.

Broward MPO. 2021. Mobility Hubs. https://www.browardmpo.org/funding-programs/mobility-hubs.

Bureau of Transportation Statistics. n.d. Effects of COVID-19 on Travel Behavior. https://www.bts.gov/browse-statistical-products-and-data/covid-related/effects-covid-19-travel-behavior.

Bureau of Transportation Statistics. 2013. 3-4 Trends in Transit Ridership: 1990–2010. https://www.bts.gov/archive/publications/pocket_guide_to_transportation/2013/system_use_and_livable_communities/figure_03_04.

California Air Resources Board. 2019. Zero-Emission Airport Shuttle Regulation Factsheet. https://ww2.arb.ca.gov/sites/default/files/2019-10/asb_reg_factsheet.pdf.

Cervero, R., S. Murphy, C. Ferrell, N. Goguts, Y. Tsai, G. B. Arrington, J. Boroski, J. Smith-Heimer, R. Golem, E. Nakajima, E. Chui, R. Dunphy, M. Myers, S. McKay, and N. Witenstein. 2004. *TCRP Report 102: Transit-Oriented Development in the United States: Experiences, Challenges, and Prospects*. Transportation Research Board, Washington, DC. https://doi.org/10.5399/osu/jtrf.47.3.2121.

Chafkin, M. 2022. Even After $100 Billion, Self-Driving Cars Are Going Nowhere. Bloomberg. https://www.bloomberg.com/news/features/2022-10-06/even-after-100-billion-self-driving-cars-are-going-nowhere.

Coffel, K., J. Parks, C. Semler, P. Ryus, D. Sampson, C. Kachadoorian, H. S. Levinson, and J. Schofer. 2012. *TCRP Report 153: Guidelines for Providing Access to Public Transportation Stations*. Transportation Research Board of the National Academies, Washington, DC.

Cohen, A, S. Shaheen, and Y. Wulff. 2024. *PAS Report 606: Planning for Advanced Air Mobility*. American Planning Association, Chicago, IL. https://www.planning.org/publications/report/9286262/.

Committee on Transportation Resilience Metrics. 2021. *TRB Special Report 340: Investing in Transportation Resilience: A Framework for Informed Choices*. Transportation Research Board, Washington, DC. https://doi.org/10.17226/26292.

Congress.gov. 2023. H.R.3935 – FAA Reauthorization Act of 2024. https://www.congress.gov/bill/118th-congress/house-bill/3935.

Coogan, M., MarketSense Consulting LLC, and Jacobs Consultancy. 2008. *ACRP Report 4: Ground Access to Major Airports by Public Transportation*. Transportation Research Board, Washington, DC. https://doi.org/10.17226/13918.

Cook, R. 2019. Pittsburgh Then and Now: The Greyhound Bus Station. *Pittsburgh Magazine*. https://www.pittsburghmagazine.com/pittsburgh-then-and-now-the-greyhound-bus-station/. Accessed August 26, 2024.

CPCS and D. Ludlow. 2019. *NCFRP Web Resource 49: Understanding and Using New Data Sources to Address Urban and Metropolitan Freight Challenges*. Transportation Research Board, Washington, DC. https://www.ncfrp49-newfreightdata.com/.

Curtis, T., M. Merritt, C. Chen, D. Perlmutter, D. Berez, and B. Ellis. 2019. *TCRP Research Report 204: Partnerships Between Transit Agencies and Transportation Network Companies (TNCs)*. Transportation Research Board, Washington, DC. https://doi.org/10.17226/25576.

Descant, S. 2023. Explosive Growth Expected Across the Micromobility Sector. Government Technology. https://www.govtech.com/fs/explosive-growth-expected-across-the-micromobility-sector.

Desilver, R. 2021. Today's Electric Vehicle Market: Slow Growth in U.S., Faster in China, Europe. Pew Research Center. https://www.pewresearch.org/short-reads/2021/06/07/todays-electric-vehicle-market-slow-growth-in-u-s-faster-in-china-europe/.

Dewberry, Gresham, Smith and Partners, GCR Inc., and R. Marchi. 2015. *ACRP Report 147: Climate Change Adaptation Planning: Risk Assessment for Airports*. Transportation Research Board, Washington, DC. https://doi.org/10.17226/23461.

Dornan, D. and J. March. 2005. *Direct User Charges*, Public Roads, Issue No: Vol. 69 No. 1. Federal Highway Administration, Washington, DC. https://highways.dot.gov/public-roads/julyaugust-2005/direct-user-charges.

Dorney, C., M. Flood, T. Grose, P. Hammond, M. Meyer, R. Miller, E. Frazier, J. Western, Y. Nakanishi, P. Auza, and J. Betak. 2021. *NCHRP Research Report 970: Mainstreaming System Resilience Concepts into Transportation Agencies: A Guide*. Transportation Research Board, Washington, DC. https://doi.org/10.17226/26125.

EBP, IBI Group, Foursquare ITP. 2022. *TCRP Research Report 235: Improving Access and Management of Public Transit ITS Data*. Transportation Research Board, Washington, DC. https://doi.org/10.17226/26674.

Emanual, G. 2024. Boston's Logan Airport Is a "De Facto Shelter" for Homeless Families. WBUR. https://www.wbur.org/news/2024/01/26/logan-airport-migrant-unhoused-shelter-emergency.

FasterCapital. n.d. Statistical Computing. https://fastercapital.com/keyword/statistical-computing.html.

Federal Aviation Administration. 2018. AC 150/5360-13A – Airport Terminal Planning. https://www.faa.gov/airports/resources/advisory_circulars/index.cfm/go/document.current/documentNumber/150_5360-13. Accessed August 28, 2024.

Federal Aviation Administration. 2023. Final CY22 Enplanements at Commercial Service Airports, by Rank Order. https://www.faa.gov/sites/faa.gov/files/2023-09/cy22-commercial-service-enplanements.pdf.

Federal Aviation Administration. 2024a. *Bipartisan Infrastructure Law-Airport Terminals Program*. Federal Aviation Administration, Washington, DC. https://www.faa.gov/bil/airport-terminals.

Federal Aviation Administration. 2024b. 2022 Airport Improvement Program (AIP) Grants. Federal Aviation Administration, Washington, DC. https://www.faa.gov/airports/aip/2022_aip_grants.

Federal Aviation Administration. 2024c. PFC Overview. https://www.faa.gov/airports/central/pfc/pfc_overview.

Federal Highway Administration. 2023a. Bipartisan Infrastructure Law Fact Sheets. Federal Highway Administration, Washington, DC. https://www.fhwa.dot.gov/bipartisan-infrastructure-law/stbg.cfm.

Federal Highway Administration. 2023b. Inflation Reduction Act Fact Sheets. Neighborhood Access and Equity (NAE) Grant Program. Federal Highway Administration, Washington, DC. https://www.fhwa.dot.gov/inflation-reduction-act/fact_sheets/nae_grant_program.cfm.

Federal Highway Administration. 2023c. Neighborhood Access and Equity (NAE) Grant Program. https://www.fhwa.dot.gov/inflation-reduction-act/fact_sheets/nae_grant_program.cfm.

Federal Highway Administration Center for Innovative Finance Support. n.d.-a. *Fact Sheets*. Federal Highway Administration, Washington, DC. https://www.fhwa.dot.gov/ipd/fact_sheets/value_cap_tax_increment_financing.aspx.

Federal Highway Administration Center for Innovative Finance Support. n.d.-b. *State Infrastructure Banks*. Federal Highway Administration, Washington, DC. https://www.fhwa.dot.gov/ipd/finance/tools_programs/federal_credit_assistance/sibs/.

Federal Railroad Administration. 2005. *Railroad Corridor Transportation Plans, A Guidance Manual*, Federal Railroad Administration, Washington, DC. https://railroads.dot.gov/sites/fra.dot.gov/files/fra_net/2751/corridor_planning.pdf. Accessed August 26, 2024.

Federal Railroad Administration. 2024. *Bipartisan Infrastructure Law Information from FRA*. Federal Railroad Administration, Washington, DC. https://railroads.dot.gov/BIL.

Federal Transit Administration. 2022a. *AASHTO Transportation Asset Management Guide*. Federal Transit Administration, Washington, DC. https://www.tam-portal.com/document/aashto-transportation-asset-management-guide-2/.

Federal Transit Administration. 2022b. *FTA Program Fact Sheets under the Bipartisan Infrastructure Law*. Federal Transit Administration, Washington, DC. https://www.transit.dot.gov/funding/grants/fta-program-fact-sheets-under-bipartisan-infrastructure-law.

Federal Transit Administration and Port Authority of NY & NJ. 2024. Port Authority Bus Terminal Replacement Project, City of New York, New York County, New York Draft Environmental Impact Statement and Draft Section 4(f) Evaluation. Federal Transit Administration, Washington, DC. https://www.panynj.gov/content /dam/bus-terminals/pabt/pabtr-deis-february-2024/draft-environmental-impact-statement/PABTR %20DEIS%20Cover%20and%20Abstract%20(PDF,%20971%20KB).pdf. Accessed August 27, 2024.

Feigon, S. and C. Murphy. 2016. *TCRP Research Report 188: Shared Mobility and the Transformation of Public Transit.* Transportation Research Board, Washington, DC. https://doi.org/10.17226/23578.

Fonseca, R. 2019. Scooters, Scooters Everywhere. Here's How LA's Grand Experiment Is Going. LAist. https://laist .com/news/las-big-scooter-experiment.

Fordham, D., J. Urrego, M. Stephens, C. Miller, B. Smith, M. Zapata, J. MacArthur, A. Rockhill, J. Greene, S. Batko, L. Bond, A. Williams, M. Crosby, and D. Culhane. 2023. *ACRP Research Report 254: Strategies to Address Homelessness at Airports.* Transportation Research Board, Washington, DC. https://doi.org/10.17226/27101.

Franzwa, D. n.d. Define Big Data. Maple Systems. https://maplesystems.com/faq/define-big-data/. Accessed August 227, 2024.

Glickman, B. 2024. Hertz Global CEO Scherr to Step Down After EV Reversal. *The Wall Street Journal.* https:// www.wsj.com/business/airlines/hertz-global-names-gil-west-as-ceo-c8080372?mod=Searchresults_pos1& page=1.

Goughnour, A., M. Albee, L. Thomas, D. Gelinne, and J. Seymour. 2020. *Pedestrian and Bicyclist Road Safety Audit (RSA) Guide and Prompt Lists.* Federal Highway Administration, Washington, DC. https://safety.fhwa .dot.gov/ped_bike/tools_solve/fhwasa12018/

Haan, K. 2023. Remote Work Statistics And Trends In 2024. Forbes Advisor. https://www.forbes.com/advisor /business/remote-work-statistics/#key_remote_work_statistics_section.

Hanlin, J., D. Reddaway, and J. Lane. 2018. *TCRP Research Report 130: Battery Electric Buses—State of the Practice.* Transportation Research Board, Washington, DC. https://doi.org/10.17226/25061.

Harding Jr., J. R., S. J. Bosch, W. P. Rayfield Jr., and J. Florie. 2017. *ACRP Research Report 177: Enhancing Airport Wayfinding for Aging Travelers and Persons with Disabilities.* Transportation Research Board, Washington, DC. https://doi.org/10.17226/24930.

Harrison, D. 2023. Bus Stations Across America Are Closing. *Wall Street Journal.* https://www.wsj.com/us-news /bus-stations-across-america-are-closing-cd2c217f.

Horadam, N. and A. Posner. 2022. *A Zero-Emission Transition for the U.S. Transit Fleet.* Federal Transit Administration, Washington, DC. https://cdn.prod.website-files.com/65031a705b5de941f4c1c742/65e795a4c33026 f8d520e203_ZE-Transition-for-US-Fleet-final-draft.pdf.

Horowitz, A. J. and N. A. Thompson. 1994. *FHWA Report: Evaluation of Intermodal Passenger Transfer Facilities.* University of Wisconsin, Milwaukee, WI. https://doi.org/10.21949/1404653.

International Transport Forum. 2018. The Shared-Use City: Managing the Curb. ITF/OECD. https://www.itf -oecd.org/shared-use-city-managing-curb-0.

InterVISTAS Consulting, Inc. Forthcoming. *ACRP Research Report 266: Airport Curbside and Terminal Area Roadway Operations: New Analysis and Strategies,* Second Edition. Transportation Research Board, Washington, DC.

Institute of Transportation Engineers. 2019. *Curbside Management Practitioners Guide.* Institute of Transportation Engineers, Washington, DC. https://www.ite.org/pub/?id=C75A6B8B-E210-5EB3-F4A6-A2FDDA8AE4AA.

ITE. n.d. Mobility Hubs Technical Brief. Available at https://www.ite.org/technical-resources/topics/complete -streets/resources/. Accessed August 26, 2024.

Kittelson & Associates, Inc., Parson Brinckerhoff, KFH Group, Inc., Texas A&M Transportation Institute, and Arup. 2013. *TCRP Research Report 165: Transit Capacity and Quality of Service Manual* (Third Edition). Transportation Research Board, Washington, DC. https://doi.org/10.17226/24766.

Landrum & Brown, Hirsh Associates, Ltd., Kimley-Horn and Associates, Inc., Jacobs Consultancy, The S-A-P Group, TransSecure, Inc., Steven Winter Associates, Inc., Star Systems, LLC, and Presentation & Design, Inc. *ACRP Report 25: Airport Passenger Terminal Planning and Design, Volume 1: Guidebook.* Transportation Research Board of the National Academies, Washington, DC, 2010. https://doi.org/10.17226/22964.

LeighFisher. 2010. *ACRP Report 40: Airport Curbside and Terminal Area Roadway Operations.* Transportation Research Board of the National Academies, Washington, DC.

Leiner, R. and T. Adler. 2020. *ACRP Research Report 215: Transportation Network Companies (TNCs): Impacts to Airport Revenues and Operations Reference Guide.* Transportation Research Board, Washington, DC. https://doi.org/10.17226/25759.

Linscott, M. and A. Posner. *TCRP Research Report 219: Guidebook for Deploying Zero-Emission Transit Buses.* Transportation Research Board, Washington, DC, 2021.

Madrigal, A. C. 2017. All the Promises Automakers Have Made About the Future of Cars. *The Atlantic.* https:// www.theatlantic.com/technology/archive/2017/07/all-the-promises-automakers-have-made-about-the-future -of-cars/532806/.

Mallela, J., P. Wheeler, G. Le Bris, and L. Nguyen. 2023. *ACRP Research Report 243: Urban Air Mobility: An Airport Perspective*. Transportation Research Board, Washington, DC. https://doi.org/10.17226/26899.

Margiotta, R., D. Krechmer, and B. Eisele. 2017. Contractor's Final Report from NCHRP Project 08-36/Task 131, Transportation Data Integration to Develop Planning Performance Measures. Cambridge Systematics, Inc. https://onlinepubs.trb.org/onlinepubs/nchrp/docs/NCHRP08-36(131)_FR.pdf.

MassDOT and MBTA. 2020a. *The MBTA Station Access Study*. MBTA, Boston, Massachusetts. https://www.mass.gov/doc/mbta-station-access-study-2020/download.

MassDOT and MBTA. 2020b. The MBTA Station Access Study. MBTA, Boston, Massachusetts.

McGeehan, P. and M. Gold. 2021. As Helicopters Fill the Skies, New Yorkers Just Want Some Peace. *The New York Times*. https://www.nytimes.com/2021/10/21/nyregion/nyc-helicopter-noise-complaints.html?searchResultPosition=13.

Merriam-Webster. n.d. Governance. https://www.merriam-webster.com/dictionary/governance.

Mitman, M., A. Rixey, T. Gibler, A. Howell, T. Swift, R. Weinberger, J. Primus, and S. Abel. 2022. *NCHRP Web Only Document 340: Dynamic Curbside Management: Keeping Pace with New and Emerging Mobility and Technology in the Public Right-of-Way*. Transportation Research Board, Washington, DC.

Molenaar, K. R., D. Alleman, A. Therrien, K. Sheeran, M. E. Asmar, and D. Papajohn. 2020. *NCHRP Research Report 939: Guidebooks for Post-Award Contract Administration for Highway Projects Delivered Using Alternative Contracting Methods, Volume 1: Design–Build Delivery*. Transportation Research Board, Washington, DC. https://doi.org/10.17226/25686.

Moody, J. and B. B. Alves. 2022. Mobility-as-a-Service (MaaS) Can Help Developing Cities Make the Most of Complex Urban Transport Systems—If They Implement It Right. World Bank Blogs. https://blogs.worldbank.org/en/transport/mobility-as-a-service-can-help-developing-cities-make-most-complex-urban-transport-systems-if-they-implement-it-right.

Morgan, C. A., J. E. Warner, E. S. Horowitz, D. P. Simpson, B. Sperry, and W. E. Zullig, Jr. *NCRRP Report 6: Guidebook for Intercity Passenger Rail Service and Development*. Transportation Research Board, Washington, DC, 2016. https://doi.org/10.17226/23535.

NACTO. 2020. 136 Million Trips Taken on Shared Bikes and Scooters Across the U.S. in 2019. https://nacto.org/2020/08/27/136-million-trips-taken-on-shared-bikes-and-scooters-across-the-u-s-in-2019/. Accessed August 25, 2024.

NACTO. 2022. *Half a Billion Trips On Shared Micromobility Since 2010*. National Association of City Transportation Officials, New York. https://nacto.org/2022/12/01/half-a-billion-rides-on-shared-bikes-and-scooters/.

National Air and Space Museum. 2021. Airline Deregulation: When Everything Changed. https://airandspace.si.edu/stories/editorial/airline-deregulation-when-everything-changed.

New Jersey Transit. n.d. Zero-Emission Buses. https://www.njtransit.com/zero-emission-buses.

NYC: The Official Website of the City of New York. 2023. Mayor Adams, NYCEDC Move to Transform Downtown Manhattan Heliport Into First-of-its-Kind Hub for Sustainable Transportation, Local Deliveries. https://www.nyc.gov/office-of-the-mayor/news/861-23/mayor-adams-nycedc-move-transform-downtown-manhattan-heliport-first-of-its-kind-hub-for#/0.

NYC Taxi and Limousine Commission. n.d. TLC Trip Record Data. https://www.nyc.gov/site/tlc/about/tlc-trip-record-data.page. Accessed August 27, 2024.

Ohnsman, A. 2022. Waymo Expanding Its Robotaxi Service To Los Angeles. Forbes. https://www.forbes.com/sites/alanohnsman/2022/10/19/waymo-expanding-its-robotaxi-service-to-los-angeles/?sh=263ba7374321.

Okunieff, P. 1997. *TCRP Synthesis 24: AVL Systems for Bus Transit*. Transportation Research Board, Washington, DC. http://www.trb.org/Publications/Blurbs/158961.aspx.

Open Mobility Foundation. 2020. What's Possible with MDS? https://www.openmobilityfoundation.org/whats-possible-with-mds/.

Parker K., J. M. Horowitz, and R. Minkin. 2022. COVID-19 Pandemic Continues To Reshape Work in America. Pew Research Center. https://www.pewresearch.org/social-trends/2022/02/16/covid-19-pandemic-continues-to-reshape-work-in-america/.

Patel, K. 2023. What Is a Dashboard? Definitions, Uses, Types, and Examples. Thoughtspot. https://www.thoughtspot.com/data-trends/dashboard/what-is-a-dashboard.

Pew Research Center. 2024. Internet, Broadband Fact Sheet. https://www.pewresearch.org/internet/fact-sheet/internet-broadband/.

Port Authority of New York and New Jersey. n.d. Midtown Bus Terminal Replacement. https://www.panynj.gov/bus-terminals/en/port-authority/planning-level-scoping-process-pabt.html.

Raine, A., J. Gast, R. Cervero, D. Belzer, and T. Poole. 2021. *TCRP Research Report 224: Guide to Joint Development for Public Transportation Agencies*. Transportation Research Board, Washington, DC. https://doi.org/10.17226/26045.

Reece, D. and T. Robinson. 2020. IATA Airport Governance Toolkit. https://www.iata.org/contentassets/fa95ede4dee24322939d396382f2f82d/iata-toolkit-on-airport-governance-a4.pdf. Accessed August 27, 2024.

Rodrigue, J.-P. 2024. *The Geography of Transport Systems*, Sixth Edition. Chapter 8: Urban Transportation. https://transportgeography.org/contents/chapter8/urban-transport-challenges/household-vehicles-united-states/.

Sam Schwartz. 2020. Visualizing the Pulse of LaGuardia Airport. https://www.samschwartz.com/staff-reflections/2020/1/30/visualizing-the-pulse-of-laguardia-airport.

SANDAG. n.d. Mobility Hubs. https://www.sandag.org/projects-and-programs/innovative-mobility/mobility-hubs.

Schwieterman, J., A. Mader, and A. Woodward. 2023. *2023 Outlook for the Intercity Bus Industry in the United States*. Chaddick's Institute, Chicago. https://las.depaul.edu/centers-and-institutes/chaddick-institute-for-metropolitan-development/research-and-publications/Documents/2023%20Outlook%20for%20the%20Intercity%20Bus%20Industry.pdf.

Seattle Department of Transportation. n.d. Free Floating Car Share Conditions of Use. https://www.seattle.gov/transportation/permits-and-services/permits/free-floating-car-share.

Shaheen, S., Cohen, A., Broader, J. Davis, R., Brown, L., Neelakantan, R., and D. Gopalakrishna. 2020a. *Mobility on Demand Planning and Implementation: Current Practices, Innovations, and Emerging Mobility Futures*. U.S. Department of Transportation, Washington, DC. https://rosap.ntl.bts.gov/view/dot/50553/dot_50553_DS1.pdf.

Shaheen, S., A. Cohen, N. Chan, and A. Bansal. 2020b. Sharing Strategies: Carsharing, Shared Micromobility (Bikesharing and Scooter Sharing), Transportation Network Companies, Microtransit, and other Innovative Mobility Modes. Elsevier, Amsterdam. https://doi.org/10.1016/B978-0-12-815167-9.00013-X.

Shared Use Mobility Center. 2023. *MaaS in Minnesota: Developing a Regional Trip Planning Platform*. Shared Use Mobility Center. https://learn.sharedusemobilitycenter.org/casestudy/maas-in-minnesota-developing-a-regional-trip-planning-platform/.

Smith, A. B. 2024. 2023: A Historic Year of U.S. Billion-Dollar Weather and Climate Disasters. https://www.climate.gov/news-features/blogs/beyond-data/2023-historic-year-us-billion-dollar-weather-and-climate-disasters. Accessed August 27, 2024.

Statista Research Department. 2024. Passengers Boarded by the Largest U.S. Air Carriers 1990–2023. https://www.statista.com/statistics/186184/passengers-boarded-by-us-air-carriers-since-1990/.

Sturgill, R. E., C. Harper, and D. Tran. 2023. *NCHRP Synthesis 605: Electric Vehicle Charging: Strategies and Programs*. Transportation Research Board, Washington, DC. https://doi.org/10.17226/27134.

SUMC. n.d. Mobility Hubs: Where People Go to Move. https://learn.sharedusemobilitycenter.org/casestudy/mobility-hubs-where-people-go-to-move-shared-use-mobility-center-2019/. Accessed January 11, 2024.

Texas Department of Transportation. 2024. ConnectSmart: Making Houston More Connected and Less Congested. https://www.txdot.gov/about/districts/houston-district/connectsmart.html.

Transportation Research Board, Committee for Review of Innovative Urban Mobility Services. 2016. *TRB Special Report 139, Between Public and Private Mobility: Examining the Rise of Technology-Enabled Transportation Services*. Transportation Research Board of the National Academies, Washington, DC. https://doi.org/10.17226/21875.

Transportation Research Board. 2024. *Critical Issues in Transportation for 2024 and Beyond*. Transportation Research Board, Washington, DC. https://nap.nationalacademies.org/catalog/27432/critical-issues-in-transportation-for-2024-and-beyond.

UN Office for Disaster Risk Reduction. 2020. *Human Cost of Disasters: An overview of the last 20 years 2000–2019*. UN Office for Disaster Risk Reduction, Geneva, Switzerland. https://www.preventionweb.net/files/74124_humancostofdisasters20002019reportu.pdf.

U.S. Department of Energy. n.d. Alternative Fuels Data Center. https://afdc.energy.gov/data.

U.S. Department of Housing and Urban Development. 2023. The 2023 Annual Homelessness Assessment Report (AHAR) to Congress. https://www.huduser.gov/portal/sites/default/files/pdf/2023-AHAR-Part-1.pdf.

U.S. Department of Transportation. n.d. ITS4US: Program Overview. https://its.dot.gov/its4us/htm/overview.htm. Accessed August 27, 2024.

U.S. Department of Transportation. 2023a. RAISE Discretionary Grants. U.S. Department of Transportation, Washington, DC. https://www.transportation.gov/RAISEgrants/about.

U.S. Department of Transportation. 2023b. Centering Equity at the U.S. Department of Transportation https://www.transportation.gov/priorities/equity/equity-strategic-goal.

U.S. Department of Transportation. 2024a. Financing. U.S. Department of Transportation, Washington, DC. https://www.transportation.gov/buildamerica/financing.

U.S. Department of Transportation. 2024b. MPDG Program. U.S. Department of Transportation, Washington, DC. https://www.transportation.gov/grants/mpdg-program.

U.S. Department of Transportation. 2024c. INFRA Grant Program. U.S. Department of Transportation, Washington, DC. https://www.transportation.gov/grants/infra-grant-program.

U.S. Department of Transportation. 2024d. Transit-Oriented Development. U.S. Department of Transportation, Washington, DC. https://www.transportation.gov/buildamerica/TOD.

U.S. Department of Transportation. 2024e. Public–Private Partnerships (P3). https://www.transportation.gov/buildamerica/p3.

U.S. Department of Transportation. 2024f. Neighborhoods Grant Program. https://www.transportation.gov/reconnecting. Accessed August 27, 2024.

U.S. Department of Transportation, Federal Railroad Administration. 2023. FY22 Corridor Identification and Development Program Selections. https://railroads.dot.gov/elibrary/fy22-CID-program-selections.

U.S. Department of Transportation Maritime Administration. 2024. *Port Infrastructure Development Program.* U.S. DOT Maritime Administration, Washington, DC. https://www.maritime.dot.gov/PIDPgrants.

U.S. Global Change Research Program. 2018. *Fourth National Climate Assessment,* U.S. Global Change Research Program, Washington, DC. https://nca2018.globalchange.gov.

U.S. Government Accountability Office. 2006. Hurricane Katrina. GAO's Preliminary Observations Regarding Preparedness, Response, and Recovery. https://www.gao.gov/assets/gao-06-442t.pdf. Accessed August 26, 2024.

U.S. Government Accountability Office. 2007. Intermodal Transportation: DOT Could Take Further Actions to Address Intermodal Barriers. GAO-07-718.

Vespa, J., L. Medina, and D. M. Armstrong. 2018. *Demographic Turning Points for the United States: Population Projections for 2020 to 2060.* U.S. Census Bureau, Washington, DC. https://www.census.gov/content/dam/Census/library/publications/2020/demo/p25-1144.pdf.

Weisbrod, G., C. Viggiano, S. Jiang, and E. Homstad. 2020. *TCRP Research Report 213: Data Sharing Guidance for Public Transit Agencies—Now and in the Future.* Transportation Research Board, Washington, DC. https://doi.org/10.17226/25696.

Willumsen, L. 2021. Use of Big Data in Transport Modelling. OECD Publishing, Paris. https://www.itf-oecd.org/big-data-transport-modelling.

WSJ Podcasts. 2023. What the WFH Revolution Means for the Economy. https://www.wsj.com/podcasts/your-money-matters/what-the-wfh-revolution-means-for-the-economy/5b66451a-cc44-4e06-b742-82b6095967d3.

Yamamoto, Z. L. 2018. Transforming the Transportation Customer Experience through Contemporary Artistic Practice: A Case Study in Strategic Implementation. *Transportation Research Record: Journal of the Transportation Research Board*, Volume 2672, Issue 8. https://doi.org/10.1177/0361198118791377.

Zapata, M., J. MacArthur, A. Rockhill, and R. Petean. 2024. *TCRP Research Report 242: Homelessness: A Guide for Public Transportation.* Transportation Research Board, Washington, DC. https://doi.org/10.17226/27248.

Acronyms and Abbreviations

AAM	Advanced Air Mobility
ADA	Americans with Disabilities Act
AIP	Airport Improvement Program
AOC	Airport Operations Center
APA	American Planning Association
API	Application Programming Interface
APTA	American Public Transit Association
ASAP	All Stations Accessibility Program
ATP	Airport Terminal Program
ATTAIN	Advanced Transportation Technologies and Innovation
AV	Automated Vehicle
AVL	Automatic Vehicle Location
BART	Bay Area Rapid Transit
BEB	Battery Electric Bus
CDS	Curb Data Specification
CFI	Charging and Fueling Infrastructure
CM/GC	Construction Management/General Contractor
CMAQ	Congestion Mitigation and Air Quality Improvement
COOP	Continuous Order of Operations Plan
CRISI	Consolidated Rail Infrastructure and Safety Improvements
CV	Connected Vehicle
DB	Design–Build
DBB	Design–Bid–Build
DBOM	Design–Build–Operate–Maintain
DEIS	Draft Environmental Impact Statement
EV	Electric Vehicle
FFY	Federal Fiscal Year
FHV	For-Hire Vehicle
GTFS	General Transit Feed Specification
HSIP	Highway Safety Improvement Program
IATA	International Air Transport Association
IIJA	Infrastructure Investment and Jobs Act
INFRA	Nationally Significant Multimodal Freight and Highway Program
ISTEA	Intermodal Surface Transportation Efficiency Act of 1991
ITE	Institute of Transportation Engineers
KPI	Key Performance Indicator
LPR	License Plate Reader
MaaS	Mobility as a Service

MARAD	Maritime Administration
MARTA	Metropolitan Atlanta Regional Transit Authority
MassDOT	Massachusetts Department of Transportation
MBTA	Massachusetts Bay Transportation Authority
MDS	Mobility Data Specification
MnDOT	Minnesota Department of Transportation
MPO	Metropolitan Planning Organization
NACTO	National Association of City Transportation Officials
NAE	Neighborhood Access and Equity
NCRRP	National Cooperative Rail Research Program
NEVI	National Electric Vehicle Infrastructure
NOFO	Notice of Funding Opportunity
NY TLC	City of New York Taxi and Limousine Commission
P3	Public–Private Partnership
PAB	Private Activity Bond
PANYNJ	Port Authority of New York and New Jersey
PAS	Planners Advisory Service
PDB	Progressive Design–Build
PFC	Passenger Facility Charge
PIDP	Port Infrastructure Development Program
RACI	Responsible Accountable Consulted Informed
RAISE	Rebuilding American Infrastructure with Sustainability and Equity
RRIF	Railroad Rehabilitation and Improvement Financing
RSA	Road Safety Audit
RTD	Regional Transit District (Denver)
SANDAG	San Diego Association of Governments
SAV	Shared Automated Vehicle
SIB	State Infrastructure Bank
SMART	Strengthening Mobility and Revolutionizing Transportation
SS4A	Safe Streets and Roads for All
SUMC	Shared Use Mobility Center
TCQSM	*Transit Capacity and Quality of Service Manual*
TIF	Tax Increment Financing
TIFIA	Transportation Infrastructure Finance and Innovation Act
TMA	Transportation Management Association
TNC	Transportation Network Company
TOD	Transit-Oriented Development
UAM	Urban Air Mobility
UN	United Nations
VTOL	Vertical Takeoff and Landing
ZEB	Zero-Emission Bus

Advanced Air Mobility: A Primer

This appendix was prepared by WSP and offers a primer on advanced air mobility (AAM). Also see *AAM* discussion in Chapter 3.

AAM is a broad term that refers to emerging aviation markets in urban, suburban, and rural communities (Cohen and Shaheen 2021). The federal government is coordinating AAM at federal level in response to the 2022 passage of the AAM Coordination and Leadership Act. U.S. DOT has formed the AAM Interagency Working Group, which is tasked with delivering an innovative and safe regulatory framework for AAM integration. The most recent FAA reauthorization defines AAM as a transportation system that is made up of urban air mobility and regional air mobility using manned or unmanned aircraft (https://www.congress.gov/bill/118th-congress/house-bill/3935).

FAA regulates AAM and has published several documents since 2020 outlining the agency's vision for AAM integration. In April 2023, FAA published the second version of *Urban Air Mobility Concept of Operations* (https://www.faa.gov/sites/faa.gov/files/Urban%20Air%20Mobility%20%20%28UAM%29%20Concept%20of%20Operations%202.0_0.pdf). This document outlines foundational principles, roles and responsibilities of various stakeholders, and operational scenarios. In July 2023, the FAA published *AAM Implementation Plan – Near-term (Innovate 28) Focus with an Eye on the Future of AAM* (https://www.faa.gov/sites/faa.gov/files/AAM-I28-Implementation-Plan.pdf). This implementation plan provides a 5-year outlook for providing information to enable AAM operations in one or more locations in the United States by 2028. Certification is expected in 2025 but not guaranteed.

The National Aeronautics and Space Administration (NASA) has orchestrated various outreach initiatives under the AAM Mission, prominently led by the AAM National Campaign, a comprehensive program designed to seamlessly integrate AAM into the National Airspace System (NAS). Serving as a testing ground for new aircraft and technologies, this campaign, conducted in collaboration with industry partners and regulatory agencies, aims to address challenges related to aircraft certification, airspace integration, and community acceptance. Concurrently, NASA has instituted AAM Ecosystem Working Groups to foster collaboration, streamline ecosystem development, and facilitate knowledge exchange among diverse stakeholder groups. This collaborative approach extends beyond technical aspects to encompass public engagement and education, emphasizing NASA's commitment to building public trust and understanding in the realm of new air transportation technologies. Further details about NASA's AAM efforts can be explored at the administration's AAM Mission website (https://www.nasa.gov/mission/aam/).

AAM serves as an umbrella term for various emerging technologies, use cases, and other terms such as urban air mobility (UAM) and regional air mobility (RAM). AAM is inclusive of both passenger and cargo transportation, including the use of small unmanned aircraft systems (UASs) for package delivery.

The use of UASs for moving human organs, blood, medical supplies, medications, food, and commercial products has grown exponentially over the past 5 years (Cornell et al. 2023). The first human organ, a kidney for transplant, was transported using a UAS in April 2019 (Coffey 2019). Zipline is a leading logistics company, leveraging UASs to increase people's access to healthcare, food, and consumer products. In 2016, Zipline began operating in Rwanda by delivering blood and other medical supplies. As of January 2024, Zipline is operating in 10 locations across the world and has successfully delivered over 892,000 packages via UAS (Zipline International Inc., 2024). Annual UAS package deliveries increased by more than 80% from 2021 to 2022, with an estimated 1 million packages delivered via UAS in 2023 (Cornell et al. 2023). NASA forecasts that up to 500 million UAS package deliveries could be happening each year by 2030 (NASA 2020).

RAM refers to using these new all-electric or hybrid aircraft or traditional aircraft with greater autonomy to provide greater regional connectivity. NASA released a report in 2021 entitled Regional Air Mobility: Leveraging Our National Investments to Energize the American Travel Experience, which defines RAM as building on and leveraging existing underutilized airport infrastructure to transport people and cargo using emerging aviation technologies that improve efficiency, affordability, and community friending integration, focused on trips between 50 to 500 miles (Antcliff et al. 2021).

UAM is a subset of AAM focusing on air transportation for people and goods in a metropolitan area (Cohen et al. 2021). Many potential use cases of this technology are being explored, including infrastructure inspections, emergency management, and—most relevant to this project—air taxis. Garrow et al. 2022 developed a taxonomy of UAM passenger aviation services that could exist in the future:

- Private service in which an aircraft would serve one individual or party;
- Air taxis, which would operate as on-demand service for a single user or single party;
- Air pooling, which would operate as on-demand service but would serve multiple individual users;
- Semi-scheduled commuter wherein departure times or locations may be subject to change based on customers' preferences and availability; and
- Scheduled commuter, which would offer frequent flights along the same route(s) in a regularly scheduled service (Garrow et al. 2022).

An additional UAM use case is an airport shuttle market "that envisions connecting AAM passenger service to, from, or between airports on fixed routes" (Goyal et al. 2021). One market demand analysis specifically analyzing the air taxi and airport shuttle markets predicted a daily passenger demand of 82,000 to be served by about 4,000 new aircraft across the United States in the most conservative scenario (Goyal et al. 2021).

Larger airports often serve as intermodal passenger facilities where rail, air, surface, and micro-transportation options often meet. AAM technologies present potential opportunities for airports large and small to increase their transportation services. *ACRP Research Report 243: Urban Air Mobility: An Airport Perspective* (Mallela et al. 2023b) provides airport professionals a guidebook and toolkit for understanding and evaluating AAM opportunities and challenges. This report provides a comprehensive market assessment, use case and applications analysis, business case considerations, AAM opportunity and impact assessments, and planning strategies for AAM integration. The report's toolkit enables professionals to determine AAM integration readiness and resources for advancing readiness for further planning.

Other intermodal ground passenger transportation facilities and organizations are also seeking to understand AAM opportunities. In November 2023, the New York City Mayor's Office and the New York City Economic Development Corporation announced the vision to update the Downtown Manhattan Heliport to include the necessary infrastructure to accommodate eVTOL aircraft and electric cargo bikes to facilitate better coordination of maritime, air, and micro-cargo delivery (City of New York – Office of the Mayor 2023).

There are studies related to AAM ground infrastructure and the associated estimated costs to retrofit existing infrastructure, such as parking garages, or to build new infrastructure to accommodate AAM aircraft (U.S. Government Accountability Office 2022). The long-term vision for UAM is to integrate the technology into other multimodal facilities, such as bus stops or metro stations. Vertiports are envisioned as part of multimodal hubs that could include transit and micromobility options.

If AAM technologies mature and operations scale, then intermodal ground passenger facilities that have not traditionally collaborated with aviation stakeholders will need to coordinate efforts to establish robust transportation ecosystems. The city of Los Angeles (LA) has been proactive in its approach to aerial transportation and planning for its adoption. *Integrating Advanced Air Mobility: A Primer for Cities* (Harper et al. 2022) captures many of the lessons learned, initiatives, and planning considerations that have been developed through LA's efforts.

Several states have also begun systematically planning for AAM adoption. Ohio was the first to publish a statewide study that analyzed AAM opportunities and use cases, primarily cargo/freight delivery, RAM, and emergency services; more information can be found in Ohio's AAM Framework (Judson et al. 2022). Utah was another leading state to conduct a systematic analysis of the state's physical and digital infrastructure that could support AAM technology. The *Utah AAM Infrastructure and Regulatory Study* (Wheeler et al. 2022) also provided a regulatory framework and resources for regional planning organizations and cities to consider while working with the State to adopt AAM.

Organizations that oversee or manage transportation facilities and infrastructure should proactively learn about AAM and its associated opportunities. Organizations can be future ready by understanding zoning considerations such as proper land use planning and airspace planning when zoning or re-zoning areas to include AAM use. Another way to be future ready is to consider the design of intermodal facilities when designing new facilities or remodeling existing infrastructure. Examine the electrical power needs of future electric vehicles and AAM electric aircraft. Consider the passenger experience and the potential movement of cargo, including small package delivery and how to plan the facility to be flexible to the adoption of these services in the future.

While great progress has been made in recent years concerning AAM and its associated technologies, there are still many unknowns. As eVTOL aircraft are certified in 2025 and begin real-world operations, more data and information will become available [FAA Research, Engineering, and Development Advisory Committee (REDAC) 2023]. As with SAVs, it is difficult to predict when some AAM use cases will reach commercial deployment or reach mature operations. It is important to understand the umbrella term of AAM and how various use cases could have significant impacts on the planning, design, and operations of intermodal passenger facilities in the future if the technology matures and scales.

References

Antcliff, K., N. Borer, S. Sartorius, P. Saleh, R. Rose, M. Gariel, J. Oldham, C. Courtin, M. Bradley, S. Roy, B. Lynch, A. Guiang, P. Stith, D. Sun, S. Ying, M. Patterson, V. Schultz, R. Ganzarski, K. Noertker, and R. Oullette. 2021, April 20. *Regional Air Mobility: Leveraging Our National Investments to Energize the American Travel Experience*. https://ntrs.nasa.gov/api/citations/20210014033/downloads/2021-04-20-RAM.pdf.

City of New York – Office of the Mayor. 2023, November 13. Mayor Adams, NYCEDC Move to Transform Downtown Manhattan Heliport Into First-of-its-Kind Hub for Sustainable Transportation, Local Deliveries. https://www.nyc.gov/office-of-the-mayor/news/861-23/mayor-adams-nycedc-move-transform-downtown-manhattan-heliport-first-of-its-kind-hub-for#/0.

Coffey, B. 2019, April 26. Special Delivery: For The First Time, Drone Flies Kidney To Patient For Successful Transplant. *General Electric News.* https://www.ge.com/news/reports/special-delivery-first-time-drone-flies -donor-kidney-patient-successful-transplant#:~:text=A%20medical%20and%20aviation%20breakthrough ,human%20kidney%20from%20Baltimore's%20St.

Cohen, A. and S. Shaheen. 2021. Urban Air Mobility: Opportunities and Obstacles. In *International Encyclopedia of Transportation.* UC Berkeley: Transportation Sustainability Research Center. https://tsrc.berkeley.edu /publications/urban-air-mobility-opportunities-and-obstacles. Accessed August 27, 2024.

Cornell, A., S. Mahan, and R. Riedel. Commercial Drone Deliveries Are Demonstrating Continued Momentum in 2023. 2023, October 6. https://www.mckinsey.com/industries/aerospace-and-defense/our-insights/future -air-mobility-blog/commercial-drone-deliveries-are-demonstrating-continued-momentum-in-2023.

Federal Aviation Administration. 2023, April 26. *Urban Air Mobility Concept of Operations V2.0.* https://www.faa .gov/sites/faa.gov/files/Urban%20Air%20Mobility%20%28UAM%29%20Concept%20of%20Operations %202.0_0.pdf.

FAA Research, Engineering, and Development Advisory Committee (REDAC). 2023, October 4. Integrating Advanced Air Mobility in the NAS. https://www.faa.gov/about/office_org/headquarters_offices/ang/redac /REDAC_AAM_generic_10042023.

Garrow, L. A., B. German, N. T. Schwab, M. D. Patterson, N. Mendonca, Y. Gawdiak, and J. R. Murphy. 2022. A Proposed Taxonomy for Advanced Air Mobility. *AIAA AVIATION 2022 Forum.* https://doi.org/10.2514 /6.2022-3321.

Goyal, R., C. Reiche, C. Fernando, and A. Cohen. 2021. Advanced Air Mobility: Demand Analysis and Market Potential of the Airport Shuttle and Air Taxi Markets. *Sustainability,* *13*(13), 7421. https://doi.org/10.3390 /su13137421.

Harper, C., S. Morrissey, and R. Pardo. 2022, December. *Integrating Advanced Air Mobility: A Primer for Cities.* https://urbanmovementlabs.org/publications/#:~:text=Integrating%20Advanced%20Air%20Mobility %3A%20A%20Primer%20for%20Cities,-December%202022&text=This%20primer%20provides%20city %20and,considerations%20for%20the%20near%20future.

Judson, F., K. Zehnder, J. Bychek, R. Del Rosario, G. Albjerg, B. Kigel, S. Kish, R. Evans, F. Gorrin-Rivas, J. Block, S. Lowry, S. Summer, and A. Guan. 2022, August. Ohio AAM Framework. https://uas.ohio.gov/about-uas /allnews/ohio+publishes+nations+first+advanced+air+mobility+framework.

Mallela, J., P. Wheeler, G. I. Bris, and L. Nguyen. 2023a. Urban Air Mobility: An airport perspective. In *Transportation Research Board eBooks.* https://doi.org/10.17226/26899.

Mallela, J., P. Wheeler, G. Le Bris, and L. Nguyen. 2023b. *ACRP Research Report 243: Urban Air Mobility: An Airport Perspective.* Transportation Research Board, Washington, DC. https://doi.org/10.17226/26899.

NASA. 2020, May. *STEM LEARNING: Advanced Air Mobility: What is AAM? Student Guide.* https://www.nasa .gov/wp-content/uploads/2020/05/what-is-aam-student-guide_0.pdf.

Public Law 117–203 117th Congress - Advanced Air Mobility Coordination and Leadership Act. 2022, October 17. Congress.gov. https://www.congress.gov/117/plaws/publ203/PLAW-117publ203.pdf.

U.S. Government Accountability Office. 2022, November. *Transforming Aviation Congress Should Clarify Certain Tax Exemptions for Advanced Air Mobility.* https://www.gao.gov/assets/gao-23-105188.pdf.

Wheeler, P., J. Mallela, G. LeBris, L. Nguyen, D. Sanchez, J. Schmidt, K. Shaw, T. Tremain, S. Atallah, S. Peterson, E. Herman, P. Dyment, and M. Dyment. 2022, December. Utah Advanced Air Mobility Infrastructure and Regulatory Study. https://www.udot.utah.gov/connect/employee-resources/uas/.

Zipline International Inc. 2024. *Building the First Logistics System that Serves all People Equally.* https://www .flyzipline.com/about.

Private Data Sources

Appendix B, a companion to Chapter 6, provides information about companies that aggregate and resell data and analytics applicable to intermodal passenger facilities.

Commercial Data and Analysis Resources

Several private companies support transportation analysis applicable to intermodal passenger facilities, including:

- Replica,
- StreetLight Data,
- INRIX, and
- Waze for Cities.

Each company's service offerings are briefly summarized in the following.

Replica

Replica provides seasonal information about the built environment in support of decision-making. According to its website, "Replica runs a seasonal, high-fidelity simulation that accurately represents the population and its travel patterns for the whole country. Customers use this data to improve planning and monitoring of transportation and land use systems, and to make decisions related to the ways people interact with the built environment" (https://documentation.replicahq.com/docs/disaggregate-trip-tables).

Replica trip data includes private automobiles, TNCs, transit, freight, and active transportation modes (walking, bicycling, and scootering). Users can view data at the census tract level, for roadway links, and for specific geographies.

StreetLight Data

StreetLight Data is a mobility analytics company that uses big data to study the movement of people, goods, and services. Streetlight offers metrics for different modes, geographies, and time ranges (https://www.streetlightdata.com/how-it-works/). The StreetLight InSight data platform contextualizes and aggregates travel patterns and provides information at the census tract level, along roadway links, and for user-drawn geographies.

INRIX

INRIX provides customers with location-based data and analytics of real-time and historical traffic and parking conditions through its INRIX IQ platform. According to its website, in addition to traffic signal and roadway data, INRIX offers curb-use analytics and provides data on parking usage patterns, including electric vehicle parking. INRIX does not provide information on walking, bicycling, or transit use.

Waze for Cities and Other Commercial Resources

Other data aggregators and consulting organizations that support data-driven decision-making are Waze for Cities, CurbIQ, Ride Report, Vianova, and Populous.ai. CurbIQ is a digital curbside management provider for digitizing curb space, compiling and analyzing usage patterns, and forecasting demand. Ride Report is a mobility management platform for bikesharing, carsharing, and scooter sharing programs. Vianova offers tools to design, operate, and analyze micromobility fleets. Populous.ai offers mobility management and curb management tools.

Project Delivery

Appendix C, a companion to Chapter 7, describes the characteristics and benefits of different models of delivering intermodal passenger facility projects, including the challenges of each. Selection of a delivery model is dependent on the unique characteristics and objectives of each project or portion of a project. Content was prepared by WSP.

Considerations When Selecting a Project Delivery Method

With a governance model in place and project planning and permitting complete (scoping, environmental evaluation and clearance, property acquisition, initial business case, and financial plan), the next step is to select a method of project delivery. As with governance models, there are numerous factors to consider including:

- Legal authority to use each delivery method.
- Risk factors, including
  - Schedule risk,
  - Project delivery timeline,
  - Cost certainty,
  - Cost overruns,
  - Politics, and
  - Extent of stakeholder collaboration required.
- Funding availability.
- Competitive environment.
- Delivery integration, including:
  - Level of contractor involvement,
  - Number of desired partnerships,
  - Limiting changes between design and construction phases, and
  - Integration of operations and maintenance.

The following section describes different infrastructure delivery methods with these considerations in mind. Additional resources on delivery methods are available through the American Association of State Highway Transportation Officials (AASHTO; https://transportation.org/) and in *NCHRP Research Report 939: Guidebooks for Post-Award Contract Administration for Highway Projects Delivered Using Alternative Contracting Methods, Volume 1: Design–Build Delivery* (Molenaar et al. 2020).

Project Delivery Methods

Design–Bid–Build

Design–bid–build (DBB) is a common method of project delivery that many government entities use. Each project phase (design and construction) is bid out sequentially through separate procurements. The public owner or project sponsor manages the interfaces between the designer and contractor. The designer develops the design and specifications to a level near 100%, and the owner uses a procurement process for the construction components. The construction contracts are bid based on 100% design drawings and specifications. In a DBB procurement, the owner assumes risks for cost and schedule. Figure C-1 illustrates the responsibilities and parties associated with a typical DBB contract.

Figure C-2 illustrates a typical sequence and breakdown of how the flow of a DBB project would progress. A scope is typically determined to bring a project to 10% design. Depending on the complexity of the project, a request for qualifications (RFQ) or a request for proposals (RFP) would follow to get to full design.

Once a designer is on board, there will be interim deliverables to bring the 10% design documents to final design. At that point in the project, the public owner would begin a traditional contractor procurement process where a general contractor would be brought on board to manage the construction work to substantial completion.

Construction Management/General Contractor

An often-used progressive delivery option is construction management/general contractor (CM/GC). This method is also known as construction manager at risk (CMAR). A CM/GC is delivered in two phases.

Phase 1: Preconstruction

CM/GC starts as the owner scopes and runs a procurement to select the designer, and the owner then conducts a procurement to select the general contractor. During Phase 1, the contractor acts as the consultant (construction manager) during the design process. The contractor

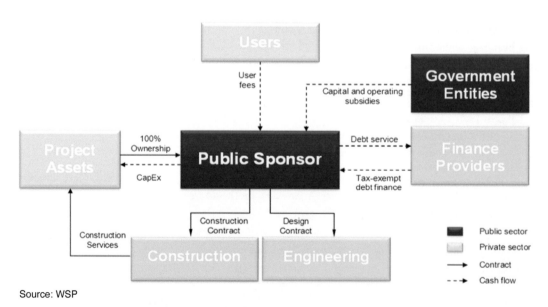

Source: WSP

Figure C-1.   Typical DBB responsibilities.

Owner

Procurement

General Contractor

Design Consultant

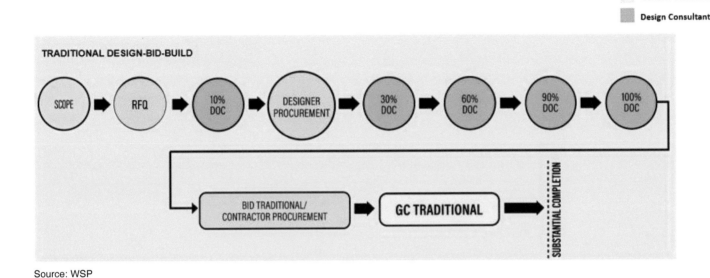

Source: WSP
Note: DOC = documents.

Figure C-2. Typical design–bid–build sequence.

offers constructability and pricing feedback on design options and identifies risks based on the contractor's established means and methods.

The owner is an active participant during the design process and can make informed decisions on design options based on the contractor's expertise.

Phase 2: Construction

Once the owner considers the design to be complete, the construction manager (CM) then has an opportunity to bid on the project based on the completed design and schedule. This is the beginning of Phase 2. If the owner, designer, and independent cost estimator agree that the contractor has submitted a fair price, the owner issues a construction contract; the CM then becomes the general contractor (https://www.fhwa.dot.gov/construction/contracts/acm/cmgc.cfm). However, this method also allows the owner to select a different general contractor if the CM submits a bid that does not meet the evaluation criteria.

Figure C-3 illustrates the relationship between the owner, the engineer, and the contractor during the two phases of CM/GC, and Figure C-4 illustrates the sequence of the two phases of CM/GC.

Design–Build

Design–build (DB) integrates different elements of delivery into a single contract. Project owners typically develop concept designs to approximately 30% and then initiate a procurement process to engage a contractor with design experience or a team that includes contractors and designers. The procurement process itself can be interactive by allowing bidding teams to propose alternative technical concepts and innovative solutions to reduce costs and accelerate the schedule.

This delivery method brings the contractor on early at the 30% level of design and transfers design and construction integration from the owner to the contractor. However, the level of design

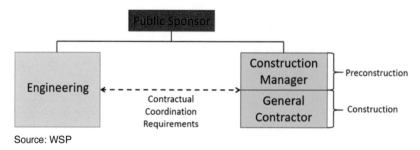

Source: WSP

Figure C-3. CM/GC relationship.

requires contractors to take a larger share of risk on unknowns because of the limited design stage. This can lead to more claims and changes for the owner if unknowns are encountered during the delivery and the risk.

The DB procurement process follows these steps:

- 30% design plans developed by owner.
- Industry review/request for industry input.
- Request for qualifications.
- Select qualified bidders.
- Issue draft RFP at approximately 30% plans with performance specifications.
- Receive bidder comments.
- One-on-one meetings held.
- Alternative technical concepts evaluated (optional).
- Final RFP issued.
- Cost and technical proposal submitted.
- Contract awarded based on best value.
- Award notice to proceed.

Figure C-5 illustrates the relationship between the parties during a typical DB project, and Figure C-6 shows the sequence of a DB delivery approach.

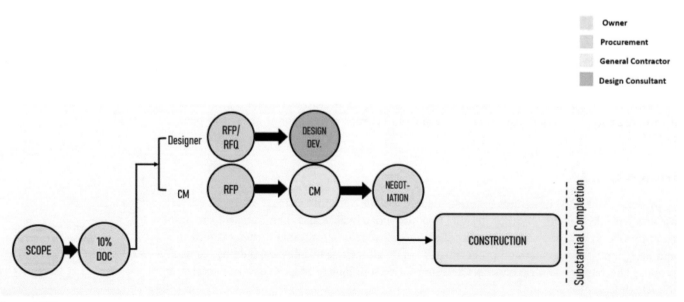

Source: WSP

Figure C-4. CM/GC phases.

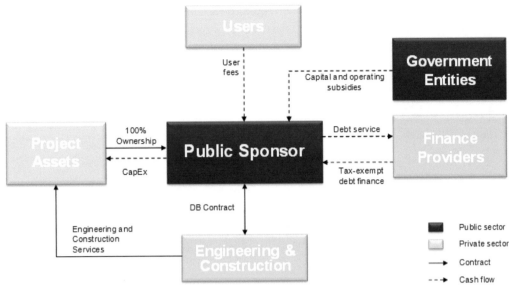

Source: WSP

Figure C-5.   DB relationships.

Progressive Design–Build

Progressive design–build (PDB) is gaining in popularity. As with CM/GC, under a PDB framework, the owner chooses a designer/builder based on qualifications. The relationship between parties is similar to that with a DB contract in that the designer is working for the contractor instead of the owner; however, the PDB includes two distinct phases: development and delivery.

A PDB delivery approach provides greater flexibility than a DB approach by defining and de-risking the project during the development phase. Once the project scope is defined to a sufficient detail, the PDP contractor then submits a hard bid for the delivery phase, which is negotiated with the owner on an open-book basis.

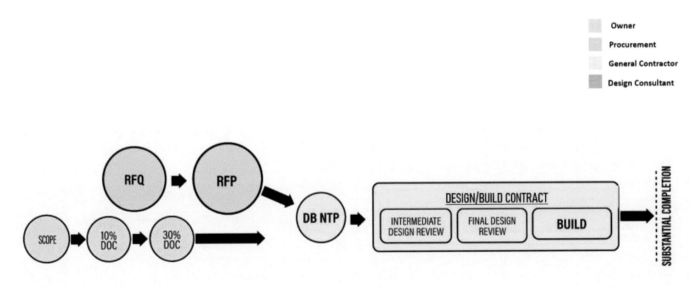

Source: WSP
Note: NTP = notice to proceed.

Figure C-6.   DB sequence of activities.

The development phase fosters an opportunity for the contractor to partner with the owner to further progress the design, determine the need for early work packages, and arrive at a more confident project cost. This method can reduce the overall delivery schedule and potential claims but has the disadvantage of the owner negotiating with a single party. Figure C-7 shows the PDB sequence.

PDB Phase Tasks

The tasks associated with each phase of a PDB option follow.

Phase 1: Development

DB services during Phase 1 are based on owner-provided design criteria and a defined scope of services, which are included with the RFP. The owner provides design criteria, basis of design documentation, and other materials, including:

- Uses,
- Space,
- Price,
- Schedule,
- Performance,
- Expandability,
- Concept design,
- Architectural guidelines,
- Design specifications,
- Standard specifications, and
- Design performance specifications.

During the proposal process, it is important for the owner to clearly define the scope and price of Phase 1 services. If the owner provides less information in the RFP, then the DB will need to develop the material during Phase 1, and Phase 1 has the potential to be open ended. Phase 1 services can be priced as cost plus, lump sum, or percentage of total project costs. The DB entity will review criteria prior to execution of the contract and confirm understanding/validity and offer innovation/changes prior to contract execution. The level of design developed during Phase 1 is dependent on the DB entity's needs for pricing Phase 2.

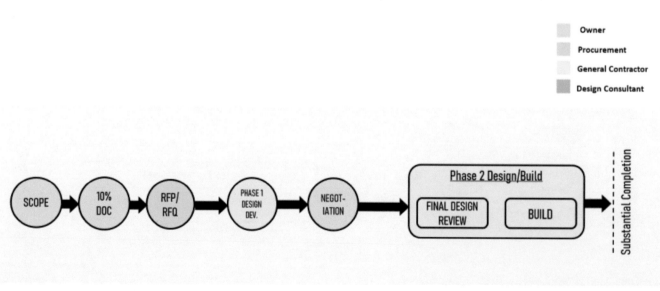

Source: WSP
Note: DOC = documents.

Figure C-7. Progressive design–build sequence.

To make sure the risks are addressed and the scope sufficiently defined, there are three general hold points in Phase 1:

- Confirmation of concept design.
- Confirmation of preliminary design.
- Confirmation of 50% design for pricing, including basis of design documents and schedule.

Phase 2: Delivery

Phase 2 is an amendment to the initial PDB contract where the cost is negotiated through open-book pricing at the conclusion of Phase 1. If the owner and the DB entity cannot reach agreement on the pricing, each has the option of exiting the agreement, and the contract is terminated.

During Phase 2, the DB entity performs final design reviews and constructs the project. The owner can lock certain terms and costs at the RFP phase of the PDB contract, which would then not be subject to renegotiation at the conclusion of Phase 1. These could include:

- Phase 1 costs,
- Contractor's overhead percentage,
- Target price,
- Substantial completion date, and
- Liquidated damages.

The contract can be terminated if no agreement is reached.

Design–Build–Operate–Maintain

In most intermodal passenger facility projects, the owner is ultimately responsible for facility operations and maintenance (O&M) and receives the facility back from the contractor once construction is complete. Under a design–build–operate–maintain (DBOM) delivery model, the same team involved with DB or PDB is also responsible for operations and maintenance over a defined period. DBOM projects typically require the contractor to meet performance measures during the O&M period to ensure that the facility is well maintained throughout the term. With a DBOM, the overall project design and selection of construction materials place greater emphasis on durability of materials to optimize life-cycle costs since the DBOM contractor is concerned with the whole life of the asset. DBOM contracts typically include risk-sharing provisions and incentives to encourage cooperation between the contractor and the owner.

This model has many advantages, including:

- O&M activities are paid for based on performance measures;
- Life-cycle concerns are considered in overall design and selection of construction materials;
- O&M can be repriced periodically;
- The facility is returned to the project sponsor at the end of the term; and
- Contracts include risk-sharing provisions and incentives to encourage cooperation between parties in a long-term partnership.

Figures C-8 and C-9 show the sequence of the DBOM and PDB with an O&M tail, respectively.

Public–Private Partnership

U.S. DOT defines a public–private partnership (P3) as a contractual agreement formed between a public agency and a private entity that allows for greater private participation in transportation project delivery and financing (U.S. Department of Transportation 2024e). All P3s include financing, operations, and maintenance.

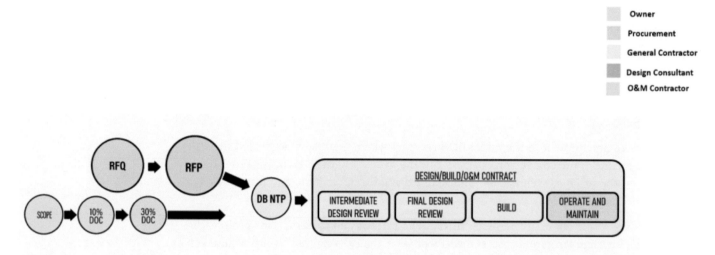

Source: WSP
Note: NTP = notice to proceed.

Figure C-8.   DBOM.

Payments under a P3 can be revenue risk, where the private partner is reimbursed with project revenue (e.g., tolls), or via availability payments, where the public owner pays the private partner back with regularly scheduled payments throughout the term. In either instance, the owner assesses liquidated damages when performance does not meet the P3 contract performance standards. The public owner can make milestone payments during the delivery phase if funds are available, thus limiting the amount of equity or financing that is required by the private sector. (See Chapter 8.)

In all cases, public sponsors procure the P3 through a transparent process that includes extensive interactions between the public owner and each private-sector proposer. The inter-actions include confidential discussions and proposals on design development (often including

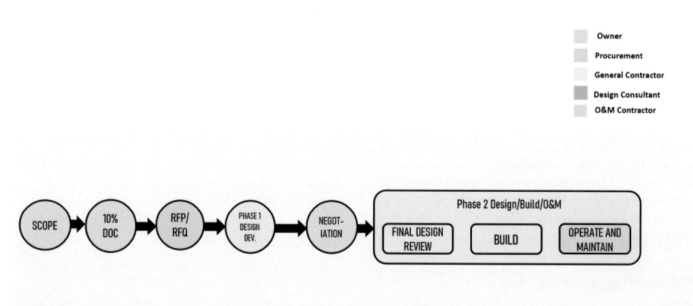

Source: WSP

Figure C-9.   Progressive DBOM with O&M tail.

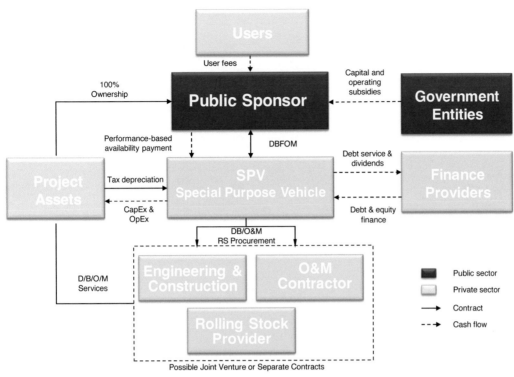

Source: WSP
Note: DBFOM = design–build–finance–operate–maintain.

Figure C-10.   Public–private partnership structure.

alternative technical concepts), interactions to negotiate risk transfer and contract terms, and financial discussions to determine the best value for the owner.

Private-sector participants form a special purpose vehicle (SPV) to integrate and deliver all aspects of the project, including design, construction, operations and maintenance, and financing, and provide a single point of contact for the public owner.

The structure for a typical availability payment type P3 is shown in Figure C-10. The public owner maintains 100% ownership of the asset and makes periodic availability payments once the construction of the asset is complete. To fully gain the value of partnership, the term of a P3 contract is usually 30 to 50 years. P3s are not a form of privatization and are not sources of funding.

The procurement of a P3 requires expertise from public owners that they may not have in-house. It is important for public owners to have competent legal, financial, and technical advisers to assist in the development of procurement documents and throughout the procurement process. A P3 contract can take more than 2 years to procure and negotiate, but the benefits of an integrated delivery with project financing and a performance-based operations and maintenance contract can outweigh the disadvantages of a lengthy procurement time frame. Figure C-11 shows the P3 sequence of activities during procurement.

Evaluating Project Delivery Models

When evaluating project delivery options, project planners and owners should determine the legal authorities available, the goals for the procurement, and how each option meets these goals, which can include cost and schedule certainty, speed of delivery, integration of services, degree

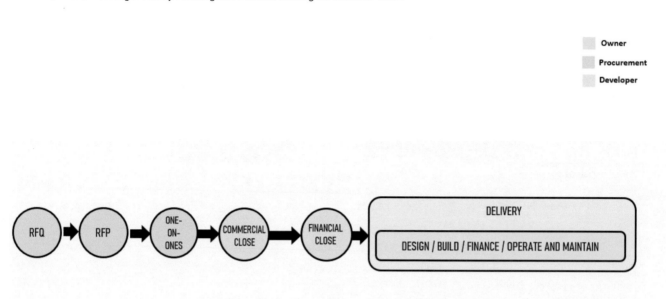

Source: WSP

Figure C-11.   Public–private partnership sequence.

of risk transfer, and compatibility with existing services available to the owner. The evaluation process is typically both qualitative and quantitative.

Qualitative Comparison of Project Delivery

A qualitative comparison can identify necessary trade-offs to achieve stakeholder consensus. For more complex intermodal passenger facility projects, more than one delivery model may be appropriate for different project elements. For example, the redevelopment of Denver Union Station and the surrounding TOD project used a P3 for the station, while a private real estate development team redeveloped the project around the station. Figure C-12 shows, by goal category, a hypothetical evaluation using the six models discussed in this chapter.

In this example, the project goal is to quickly deliver a facility funded through facility revenue and downstream grants. The qualitative analysis indicates P3 as the most promising delivery model. P3 works in this instance because of the project's accelerated schedule; the ability to meet the funding profile; the integration of design, construction, and operations and maintenance; the ability to enhance innovation; and price and schedule certainty. A PDB delivery option also scores well but does not include operations and maintenance services.

Quantitative Analysis of Project Delivery Options

Following the qualitative evaluation, a quantitative analysis can be used to refine the most promising options to evaluate specific project risk assessments, update cost estimates, compare schedules, and evaluate conceptual financing plans for each delivery model. It is important that the analysis receive input from identified stakeholders and that they understand their roles and responsibilities and how each delivery model will affect their workstreams and overall project governance.

Table C-1 shows the overall approach to the selection of a delivery method, including both qualitative and quantitative analysis.

GOALS / DELIVERY METHOD	DESIGN-BID-BUILD	CM/GC	DESIGN-BUILD	PROGRESSIVE DESIGN-BUILD	DBOM	PUBLIC-PRIVATE PARTNERSHIP (P3)
Meet aggressive schedule	○ (empty)	◐ (half)	◕ (¾)	● (full)	◕ (¾)	● (full)
Provide early cost certainty	○ (empty)	◔ (¼)	● (full)	◕ (¾)	● (full)	◕ (¾)
Minimize risk of cost overruns	◕ (¾)	◕ (¾)	◐ (half)	◕ (¾)	◐ (half)	◕ (¾)
Maximize stakeholder collaboration	● (full)	◕ (¾)	◐ (half)	● (full)	◐ (half)	◕ (¾)
Allow phased funding	◐ (half)	● (full)	○ (empty)	● (full)	○ (empty)	● (full)
Maximize competition among bidders	● (full)	○ (empty)	● (full)	○ (empty)	● (full)	○ (empty)
Allow contractor involvement / innovation	○ (empty)	● (full)	◕ (¾)	● (full)	◕ (¾)	● (full)
Maximize partnership opportunities	○ (empty)	● (full)	◐ (half)	● (full)	◐ (half)	● (full)
Limit changes between design and construction	○ (empty)	◐ (half)	● (full)	◕ (¾)	● (full)	● (full)
Integrate operations & maintenance	○ (empty)	○ (empty)	○ (empty)	○ (empty)	● (full)	● (full)

Most favorable > ● ◕ ◐ ◔ ○ < Least favorable

Figure C-12.   Hypothetical qualitative comparison of project delivery methods.

Source: WSP

Table C-1.   Qualitative and quantitative analysis of project delivery methods.

Qualitative Analysis		Quantitative Analysis	
Options	Constraints	Feasibility study	Preferred option
Procurement method	Stakeholder objectives	Refinement of cost and revenue estimates	Variation over phases
Project scope	Market appetite	Risk analysis	Risk allocation
Phasing	Potential public funds	Financial structure	Governance
	Legal	Value of options comparison	Legal changes
	Regulatory		Range of funding need

Source: WSP

APPENDIX D

Federal Funding

Appendix D, a companion to Chapter 8, describes each federal funding program and includes detailed tables of matching requirements, eligibility, funding amounts through FY 2026, and typical award size. Readers are also encouraged to consult the U.S. DOT website for current information on grant programs (https://www.transportation.gov/grants).

General Formula and Grant Programs

Table D-1 presents an overview of the program type, matching requirements, eligibility, funding amount through FY 2026, and typical award size for each of the general programs. General programs can utilize funding for a variety of multimodal transportation projects and, overall, provide the greatest range of eligible activities of the program types. Moreover, seven of the nine general programs can be used to fund the planning, design, or construction phase of a project. The general programs are split between four formula programs and five discretionary grant programs.

FHWA Surface Transportation Block Grant Program

FHWA distributes Surface Transportation Block Grant (STBG) funds to states and metropolitan planning organizations (MPOs) using a highway-based funding formula. STBG is a flexible funding source for a range of transportation projects. Newly eligible activities added through the IIJA include projects that facilitate intermodal connections between emerging transportation technologies, electric vehicle (EV) charging infrastructure projects, and projects for the construction of bus rapid transit corridors.

The STBG is the most well-funded of the general funding programs applicable to intermodal passenger facilities, with the IIJA allocating a little over $14 billion in STBG funding annually through 2026. Nearly every aspect of planning, designing, and constructing an intermodal passenger facility qualifies for funding from the STBG program. STBG guidance specifically highlights multimodal projects that improve public transportation access, including transit capital projects, pedestrian and bicycle projects, and ferry boat and terminal projects.

FHWA Congestion Mitigation and Air Quality Program

FHWA administers the Congestion Mitigation and Air Quality (CMAQ) program with an approximate total of $2.5 billion in annual funding apportioned as a lump sum among the states. CMAQ funds transportation projects and programs to reduce congestion and improve air quality in designated air quality maintenance or non-attainment areas for carbon monoxide or ozone. The IIJA expanded the eligible activities for the CMAQ program to include shared mobility (e.g., bikeshare and scooter share).

Table D-1. General formula and grant program matrix.

Funding Program	Type	Local Match	Eligibility								FY 23–26 Funding	Typical Award Size
			Planning	Design	Construction	Stations	Transit vehicles	EV Charging	Road/Bike/Ped	Airports/Ports		
FHWA Surface Transportation	Formula	Federal share ≤ 80% of total project cost (≤ 90% for projects on interstate system)	✓	✓	✓	✓	✓	✓	✓	✓	$58 billion	n/a, distributed to states
FHWA Congestion Mitigation and Air Quality Improvement (CMAQ)	Grant	Federal share ≤ 80% of total project cost	✓	✓	✓	✓	✓	✓	✓		$10.7 billion	n/a, distributed to states
DOT Rebuilding American Infrastructure with Sustainability and Equity (RAISE)	Grant	Federal share ≤ 80% of total project costs	✓	✓	✓	✓	✓	✓	✓	✓	$6.0 billion	Max. award = $25 million
FHWA Carbon Reduction Program	Formula	Typically; federal share = 80% (= 90% for projects on interstate system)	✓	✓	✓	✓	✓	✓	✓	✓	$5.2 billion	n/a, distributed to states
DOT National Infrastructure Project Assistance (MEGA)	Grant	Federal share ≤ 80%, MEGA share ≤ 60%	✓	✓	✓	✓			✓	✓	$4 billion	None
DOT Rural Surface Transportation	Grant	Federal share ≤ 100%, rural share ≤ 80%	✓	✓	✓				✓		$1.6 billion	None
FTA Sections 5303, 5304, and 5305	Formula	Federal share ≤ 80% of total project costs	✓			✓			✓		$780 million	n/a, distributed to states
DOT Strengthening Mobility and Revolutionizing Transportation (SMART)	Grant	No requirement	✓	✓	✓				✓	✓	$400 million	Max. award = $2 million
FTA Transit-Oriented Development (TOD) Planning Program	Grant	Federal share ≤ 80% of total project costs	✓			✓			✓		$55 million	Max. grant = $1.6 million

Note: n/a = not applicable.

CMAQ funding levels are based on the population in the non-attainment and maintenance areas of the state and the severity of air quality ratings. By formula, CMAQ funding levels increase to address worsening regional air quality ratings. Quantifying the ability to reduce congestion and improve air quality in the region allows intermodal passenger facilities to leverage CMAQ funding. Transit facilities (e.g., stations, terminals, transfer facilities) are highlighted as an eligible category in the CMAQ guidance, along with new transit vehicles (e.g., diesel engine retrofits). Constructing bicycle and pedestrian facilities and installing traffic calming measures are also among the eligible activities that intermodal passenger facilities qualify for.

U.S. DOT Rebuilding American Infrastructure with Sustainability and Equity Grant Program

The Rebuilding American Infrastructure with Sustainability and Equity (RAISE) grant program, formerly known as BUILD or TIGER, is a highly competitive DOT grant program. RAISE supports the capital costs of road, rail, transit, and multimodal projects that have a significant impact on the nation, a region, or a metropolitan area.

The RAISE program is extremely competitive. Broad support and local consensus, including support from the business community, various interest groups (e.g., environmental, labor, economic development), and elected officials at the federal, state, and local levels are key requirements to being competitively positioned for RAISE funding. DOT also prefers projects that have completed considerable project development (e.g., finalized environmental clearance) and secured commitments of matching non-federal funding.

The eligible project categories relevant to intermodal passenger facilities include public transportation, passenger and freight rail, port infrastructure, and surface transportation components of an airport project.

FHWA Carbon Reduction Program

The Carbon Reduction program was established by the IIJA as a formula grant program to states to reduce transportation emissions or aid in the development of carbon reduction strategies. The IIJA has apportioned approximately $1.3 billion annually to this program through FY 2026.

Intermodal passenger facilities qualify for funding from the Carbon Reduction program under several eligible activities. Eligible public transportation projects include bus rapid transit corridors and bus passenger loading facilities. Moreover, projects for on- and off-road trail facilities for pedestrians, bicyclists, and other nonmotorized forms of transportation qualify and may include shared mobility projects. The construction and operation of zero-emission vehicle charging infrastructure are also included as part of the program.

U.S. DOT National Infrastructure Project Assistance Program

The National Infrastructure Project Assistance grant program, commonly referred to as MEGA, was created to support large projects that are difficult to fund even though they provide national or regional economic, mobility, or safety benefits. This new program was enacted as part of the IIJA. DOT announced that $1 billion will be made available annually through FY 2026. Fifty percent of funds were made available for projects greater than $500 million and 50% for projects between $100 million and $500 million in cost.

MEGA is now part of the Multimodal Project Discretionary Grant (MPDG) opportunity, which is a combined solicitation. The other grant programs included in the MPDG are the

Nationally Significant Multimodal Freight & Highway Projects grant program (INFRA) and the Rural Surface Transportation grant program. MPDG allows applicants to apply to one, two, or all three of these funding opportunities by submitting only one application.

To be applicable for a MEGA grant, projects must:

- Generate national or regional economic, mobility, or safety benefits;
- Demonstrate significant need of federal funding;
- Be cost-effective;
- Have a stable and dependable funding source available to pay for O&M costs through the project life; and
- Show that the applicant has sufficient legal, financial, and technical capacity to carry out the project.

Intermodal passenger facility projects can capitalize on the multimodal focus of MEGA and the MPDG. Public transportation projects only qualify for a MEGA grant if incorporated with any of the following project types: a highway or bridge project on the National Highway Freight Network/National Highway System, a freight intermodal/rail project, a railway highway grade separation/elimination project, or an intercity passenger rail project.

U.S. DOT Rural Surface Transportation Grant Program

The Rural Surface Transportation grant program supports projects that increase connectivity and improve safety and reliability of the infrastructure in rural areas. A project is designated as rural if it is an urban area of less than 200,000 people or is fully outside any urban area.

This competitive program is part of the MPDG opportunity, which is a combined solicitation. The other grant programs included in the MPDG are MEGA and INFRA. MPDG allows applicants to apply to one, two, or all three of these funding opportunities by submitting only one application. The Rural Surface Transportation grant program can only cover 80% of eligible project costs. However, other federal sources can be used for the non-rural match. This means projects can be funded 100% through federal funds if multiple federal funding sources are used.

Eligibility for intermodal passenger facilities is limited with the rural program. Passenger facilities could potentially see benefit tangentially from any project on a publicly owned highway or bridge that provides or increases access to an intermodal facility that supports the economy of a rural area.

FTA Sections 5303, 5304, and 5305

The Metropolitan & Statewide Planning and Non-Metropolitan Transportation Planning programs provide formula-based federal grants for multimodal transportation planning. Funding is apportioned to state DOTs that then allocate funding to MPOs. The funds should result in long-range plans as well as short-term programs that reflect a state's transportation priorities.

The Metropolitan & Statewide Planning and Non-Metropolitan Transportation Planning programs are aimed toward planning activities that support economic vitality, increase safety, increase the security of the transportation system, increase accessibility and mobility, enhance connectivity, and preserve existing transportation systems. Intermodal passenger facilities fall squarely under these eligible activities, and applicants can use funding for planning for intermodal passenger facilities as part of their short-term and long-term transportation goals.

U.S. DOT Strengthening Mobility and Revolutionizing Transportation Grant Program

The Strengthening Mobility and Revolutionizing Transportation (SMART) grant program provides discretionary grants to help drive technology innovations in transportation. This program was introduced as part of the IIJA, which authorized $100 million annually in competitive grants through 2026.

The U.S. DOT notes that priority will be given to projects focused on advanced smart city or community technologies and systems to improve transportation efficiency and safety. The focus on technological innovations means that intermodal passenger facilities can use SMART funding for related projects such as implementing mobility as a service, last-mile service through shared connected and automated vehicles, urban air mobility, transit priority signaling, and other sensor-based technologies that improve pedestrian and cyclist accessibility (e.g., on-demand conversion of right-of-way for pedestrians and cyclists, sensor-based shared streets, and zero-emission zones).

FTA Pilot Program for Transit-Oriented Development Planning

FTA's Pilot Program for Transit Oriented Development Planning offers discretionary grants to promote growth around transit stations to create compact, mixed-use communities with easy access to jobs and services. The program provides funding to integrate land use and transportation planning in conjunction with a project that seeks funding through the FTA's Capital Investment Grants program. The pilot program was continued by the IIJA, with $13 million to $14 million in funding available annually through 2026.

One of the main goals of the program is to improve ridership by fostering multimodal connectivity and accessibility. The program funds planning efforts for increasing pedestrian and bicycle access to transit stations, as well as fostering development around existing intermodal passenger facilities. Intermodal passenger facilities could also use funding from the program to identify opportunities for public–private partnerships.

Vehicle Funding Programs

Programs under the vehicles category support intermodal passenger facilities by providing formula and discretionary grant funding for transit zero-emission fleet acquisition, facilities/stations supporting zero-emission transit vehicles, and EV charging infrastructure. Table D-2 provides a general overview of the program type, matching requirements, eligible activities, funding amount through FY 2026, and typical award size of grants for the vehicle programs. While this report focuses specifically on facilities, some of the federal funding programs listed in this section may assist with elements of an intermodal facility expansion, such as vehicle procurement and charging/fueling infrastructure.

FTA Section 5339 (a), (b), and (c)

FTA Section 5339 is made up of three programs for buses and bus facilities. Intermodal passenger facilities with bus service can capitalize on the significantly higher funding levels for these three programs thanks to the IIJA. While 5339 (a) is a formula funding program, 5339 (b) and (c) are discretionary grant programs (Federal Transit Administration 2022b).

Section 5339 (a) and (b) provides funding for states and transit agencies to purchase buses and replace, rehabilitate, and construct bus-related facilities, including technological changes or

Table D-2. Vehicle funding matrix.

Funding Program	Type	Local Match	Eligibility								FY23–26 Funding	Typical Award Size
			Planning	Design	Construction	Stations	Transit vehicles	EV Charging	Road/Bike/Ped	Airports/Ports		
FTA Section 5339 (a), (b), and (c)	Formula/grant	Federal share ≤ 80% of total project costs	✓	✓	✓	✓	✓				$6.5 billion	Max. award to date = $116 million
FHWA National Electric Vehicle Infrastructure (NEVI) Formula Program	Formula	Federal share ≤ 80% of total project costs	✓	✓	✓			✓			$4.0 billion	n/a, distributed to states
FHWA Charging and Fueling Infrastructure (CFI) Discretionary Grant Program	Grant	Federal share ≤ 80% of total project costs	✓	✓	✓			✓			$2.2 billion	Max. award = $15 million for community, no max. for corridor projects
FTA Ferry Programs	Grant	Federal share ≤ 80% of total project costs (≤ 85% for vehicles, ≤ 90% for vehicle-related equipment/facilities, ADA compliance)		✓	✓	✓	✓		✓	✓	$1.2 billion+	Max. award in FFY 22 = $72 million

Note: n/a = not applicable.

innovations to modify low- or no-emission vehicles or facilities. Section 5339 (a) allocates more than $600 million annually through 2026 to states and transit agencies; intermodal passenger facilities can leverage these formula funds in addition to the approximately $400 million annually distributed through the 5339 (b) grant program. Applications for the competitive discretionary program, Section 5339 (b), are evaluated based on demonstration of need or the quality and extent to which the proposer demonstrates how the proposed project will address the need for capital investment in bus vehicles or supporting facilities. Applications are also assessed based on demonstration of benefits, how the proposed project will improve the condition of the transit system, how it will improve the reliability of transit service for its riders, and how it will enhance access and mobility within the service area. While the maximum federal share of net project costs is 80% under this program, grants directed to helping individuals with disabilities may be able to secure a higher federal share for certain projects (Federal Transit Administration 2022b).

Section 5339 (c) provides grant funding to state and local governmental authorities for the purchase or lease of zero-emission and low-emission transit buses as well as the acquisition, construction, and leasing of required supporting facilities. Eligible supporting facilities include recharging and refueling facilities for zero-/low-emission buses at intermodal passenger facilities. All applicants requesting funding for zero-emission-vehicle–related projects must include a single Zero-Emission Transition plan document containing the following information, at a minimum:

- Demonstrate a long-term fleet management plan with a strategy for how the applicant intends to use the current request for resources and future acquisitions.
- Address the availability of current and future resources to meet costs for the transition and implementation.
- Consider policy and legislation affecting relevant technologies.
- Include an evaluation of existing and future facilities and their relationship to the technology transition.
- Describe the partnership of the applicant with the utility or alternative fuel provider.
- Examine the impact of the transition on the applicant's current workforce by identifying skill gaps, training needs, and retraining needs of the existing workers of the applicant to operate and maintain zero-emission vehicles and related infrastructure and avoid displacement of the existing workforce (Federal Transit Administration 2022b).

FHWA National Electric Vehicle Infrastructure Formula Program

The National Electric Vehicle Infrastructure (NEVI) Formula Program will provide formula grants to states to strategically deploy EV charging infrastructure and to establish an interconnected network to facilitate data collection, access, and reliability. This is a new program that was enacted as part of the IIJA, unlocking $1 billion annually in funding through 2026. While NEVI is primarily a formulaic program, the program sets aside 10% of funds for discretionary grants to assist state and local governments in strategically deploying electric vehicle charging infrastructure (Federal Highway Administration 2023a).

Each state DOT must submit a plan to U.S. DOT describing how NEVI formula funds will be used before it can access and apportion funds to local entities. The plan will detail locations for charging infrastructure on one of the state's designated alternative fuel corridors. Intermodal passenger facilities located on these alternative fuel corridors qualify for NEVI formula funding. In addition to funding the acquisition and installation of EV charging infrastructure, NEVI will help with operations and maintenance of infrastructure previously acquired through the program. Other eligible projects include analysis to evaluate the demand for EV charging infrastructure, data sharing about EV charging infrastructure, and traffic control devices to provide directions to acquired EV charging infrastructure (Federal Highway Administration 2023a).

FHWA Charging and Fueling Infrastructure Discretionary Grant Program

The Charging and Fueling Infrastructure (CFI) Discretionary Grant Program is a new competitive grant program created by the IIJA. Owners of intermodal passenger facilities looking to add electric vehicle charging stations should consider the CFI program since it provides $400 to $700 million per year in discretionary grant funding through 2026. The CFI program has two tracks for applications:

- **Corridor charging:** To deploy EV charging and hydrogen/propane/natural gas fueling infrastructure along designated alternative fuel corridors.
- **Community charging:** To install EV charging and alternative fuel along public roads and in schools, parks, and public parking facilities.

Special priority is given to projects located in low (and moderate) income neighborhoods as well as in rural areas (Federal Highway Administration 2023a).

FTA Ferry Program

The FTA Ferry Program is a set of three competitive grant programs distributed by the FTA. Intermodal passenger facilities with passenger ferry components can utilize these three programs to improve and expand passenger ferry service (Federal Transit Administration 2022b).

The Passenger Ferry Grant Program is set to receive $30 million annually through FY 2026. The program supports passenger ferry systems in urbanized areas. Capital projects, such as the acquisition, replacement, or rehabilitation of ferries, terminals, and other facilities and equipment, are eligible for funding. Competitiveness for the program depends on factors such as age and condition of ferries, terminals, and other infrastructure; rider benefits; project readiness; and connectivity to other modes. An important note is that passenger ferry grants cannot be used for operating, planning, or preventative maintenance expenses (Federal Transit Administration 2022b).

The Electric or Low-Emitting Ferry Pilot Program is a new program created by the BIL. It is set to receive $50 million annually through FY 2026, with an additional $50 million per year in advance appropriations, for a total of up to $100 million per year. Ferry vessels that reduce emissions through alternative fuels or onboard energy systems, along with necessary charging infrastructure, qualify for this program (Federal Transit Administration 2022b).

The Ferry Service for Rural Communities Program is the rural-focused counterpart to the Passenger Ferry Grant Program; $200 million per year is authorized for the program through 2026, with an additional $200 million in advance appropriations annually. Eligible activities include capital, planning, and operating assistance for regularly scheduled ferry service. To qualify for the Rural Communities Program, the ferry system must serve two or more rural areas located 50 or more sailing miles apart or serving two rural areas with a single segment over 20 miles between two rural areas that otherwise does not qualify for the Passenger Ferry Grant Program (Federal Transit Administration 2022b).

Roadway Funding Programs

Roadway funding programs support the development of bicycle, pedestrian, and road infrastructure surrounding intermodal passenger facilities. Table D-3 provides a general overview of the program type, matching requirements, eligible activities, funding amount through FY 2026, and typical award size of roadway program grants.

Table D-3. Roadway program funding matrix.

Funding Program	Type	Local Match	Eligibility								FY 23–26 Funding	Typical Award Size
			Planning	Design	Construction	Stations	Transit vehicles	EV Charging	Road/Bike/Ped	Airports/Ports		
FHWA Surface Transportation	Formula	Federal share ≤80% of total project cost (≤90% for projects on interstate system)	✓	✓	✓	✓	✓	✓	✓	✓	$58 billion	n/a, distributed to states
FHWA Congestion Mitigation and Air Quality Improvement (CMAQ)	Grant	Federal share ≤80% of total project cost	✓	✓	✓		✓	✓	✓		$10.7 billion	n/a, distributed to states
DOT Rebuilding American Infrastructure with Sustainability and Equity (RAISE)	Grant	Federal share ≤80% of total project costs	✓	✓	✓	✓	✓	✓	✓	✓	$6.0 billion	Max. award = $25 million
FHWA Carbon Reduction program	Formula	Typically: federal share = 80% (= 90% for projects on interstate system)	✓	✓	✓	✓	✓	✓	✓	✓	$5.2 billion	n/a, distributed to states
DOT National Infrastructure Project Assistance (MEGA)	Grant	Federal share ≤80%, MEGA share ≤60%	✓	✓	✓	✓			✓	✓	$4 billion	None
DOT Rural Surface Transportation	Grant	Federal share ≤100%, rural share ≤80%	✓	✓	✓				✓		$1.6 billion	None
FTA Sections 5303, 5304, and 5305	Formula	Federal share ≤80% of total project costs	✓			✓			✓		$780 million	n/a, distributed to states
DOT Strengthening Mobility and Revolutionizing Transportation (SMART)	Grant	No requirement	✓	✓	✓				✓	✓	$400 million	Max. award = $2 million
FTA Transit-Oriented Development (TOD) Planning Program	Grant	Federal share ≤80% of total project costs	✓			✓			✓		$55 million	Max. grant = $1.6 million

Note: n/a = not applicable.

FHWA Highway Safety Improvement Program

The Highway Safety Improvement Program (HSIP) provides formula funding from the FHWA for the reduction of traffic fatalities and serious injuries on all public roads. Applicants to the HSIP must focus on performance and demonstrate a data-driven, strategic approach to improving highway safety. The IIJA ensures that HSIP will receive up to $3+ billion annually through 2026 to allocate to states (Federal Highway Administration 2023a).

Thanks to the IIJA, new eligible activities make the HSIP more relevant than ever for intermodal passenger facilities. The IIJA specifies that HSIP can be utilized for traffic calming measures and roadway improvements that separate motor vehicles from pedestrians and bicyclists. Moreover, up to 50% of HSIP apportionments can be transferred at the state's discretion to other funding programs that intermodal passenger facilities could tap into. Programs that HSIP funding could be transferred to include the STBG program, the CMAQ Program, and the Carbon Reduction Program (Federal Highway Administration 2023a).

U.S. DOT Nationally Significant Multimodal Freight and Highway Program

The Nationally Significant Multimodal Freight & Highway Projects Grant program (also known as INFRA) is dedicated to rebuilding the nation's aging infrastructure. INFRA utilizes selection criteria that promote projects that are critical to national and regional economic vitality as well as environmental justice goals toward highway and intercity/freight rail projects. The program also incentivizes project sponsors to pursue innovative delivery strategies, including public–private partnerships (U.S. Department of Transportation 2024b).

INFRA is now part of the MPDG opportunity, which is a combined solicitation. The other grant programs included in the MPDG are MEGA and the Rural Surface Transportation Grant program. MPDG allows applicants to apply to one, two, or all three of these funding opportunities by submitting only one application. INFRA grants can cover up to 60% of future eligible project costs. While INFRA grants are intended to provide funding to projects that are shovel ready and result in construction, eligible activities include planning, feasibility analysis, and revenue forecasting (U.S. Department of Transportation 2024b).

The INFRA grant program has the following goals, which factor heavily into merit criteria scoring:

- Support national and regional activity.
- Focus on climate change and environmental justice impacts.
- Advance racial equity.
- Engage more non-federal sources of infrastructure investment.
- Use innovative solutions for all aspects of the project (U.S. Department of Transportation 2024b).

INFRA's focus on freight limits some of its applicability to intermodal passenger facilities. Nonetheless, eligible project types for INFRA funding include highway freight projects, bridge projects, intermodal rail projects, and port projects. Elements of these projects can benefit intermodal passenger facilities, such as improvements to pedestrian and cyclist infrastructure or the establishment of a bus rapid transit infrastructure (U.S. Department of Transportation 2024b).

U.S. DOT Safe Streets and Roads for All Grant Program

The Safe Streets and Roads for All (SS4A) grant program is a discretionary grant program for improving roadway safety by significantly reducing or eliminating roadway fatalities and serious injuries through safety action plan development and implementation focused on all users, including pedestrians, bicyclists, public transportation users, motorists, personal conveyance and micromobility users, and commercial vehicle operators. This is a new program that was enacted as part of the IIJA, which authorized $1 billion in competitive grants per year through 2026 and an additional $200 million annually subject to future appropriation (Federal Highway Administration 2023a).

The SS4A program provides two types of grants. Planning and Demonstration Grants provide funds to develop, complete, or supplement a comprehensive safety action plan that will prevent serious injuries and roadway fatalities. Implementation Grants, on the other hand, provide funding to implement strategies and projects that are consistent with an existing action plan. SS4A grants can target a designated neighborhood or well-used public transportation route to identify and correct common risks, such as through improved pedestrian infrastructure and signage at transit stops. SS4A highlights that it supports the creation of safe routes to public transit services for pedestrians and cyclists alike (Federal Highway Administration 2023a).

U.S. DOT Neighborhood Access and Equity Grant Program

The Neighborhood Access and Equity (NAE) Grant Program was established in 2022 by the Inflation Reduction Act (IRA) to provide competitive awards to connect communities through improved walkability and safety, as well as through affordable transportation access. The NAE program shares many characteristics with the Reconnecting Communities Pilot, paired in one combined solicitation called the Reconnecting Communities and Neighborhoods (RCN) Program (Federal Highway Administration 2023c).

There are two primary types of facilities that qualify for NAE funding:

- A dividing facility is a surface transportation facility creating an obstacle to community connectivity. Key design factors include grade separation and high speeds.
- A burdening facility is a surface transportation facility that burdens a disadvantaged or underserved community, bringing negative impacts such as air pollution, noise, or stormwater (Federal Highway Administration 2023c).

The NAE received significantly more funding than the Reconnecting Communities Pilot, with $3.2 billion allocated through 2026; 40% of funding ($1.262 billion) is dedicated to economically disadvantaged communities. There are three types of grants in the NAE program:

- Community Planning Grants are dedicated to innovative community planning addressing localized transportation challenges. Up to $135 million will be awarded for Community Planning Grants through 2026.
- Capital Construction Grants can be used for the removal, retrofit, or mitigation of dividing and burdening facilities. Up to $2.57 billion in funding is set aside for Capital Construction Grants.
- Regional Partnerships Challenge Grants offer up to $450 million in funding; these grants can be used for projects addressing a persistent regional challenge in equitable access and mobility (Federal Highway Administration 2023c).

Eligible applicants include nonprofit organizations and institutions of higher education that are in partnership with local, regional, state, or tribal governments (Federal Highway Administration 2023c).

Intermodal passenger facility projects stand to benefit greatly from NAE funding. The NAE prioritizes providing affordable access to transportation links, whether through complete streets, highway caps, or active transportation networks. Intermodal passenger facilities fulfill the NAE's goal to mitigate the negative environmental impacts of the built environment through the reduction of transportation-related emissions and air pollution. Moreover, NAE funding can be used to create natural infrastructure mitigating the urban heat island effect and to manage stormwater runoff around intermodal passenger facilities. Intermodal passenger facility projects often necessitate multiple partners and stakeholders, which is encouraged by the NAE through Regional Partnerships Challenge Grants (Federal Highway Administration 2023c).

U.S. DOT Reconnecting Communities Pilot Program

The Reconnecting Communities Pilot (RCP) Program was established by the IIJA as the first-ever federal program dedicated to amending the burdens of past transportation infrastructure decisions and to reconnecting communities that were cut off from each other. The IIJA dedicates $200 million annually in grants to the RCP program, $50 million of which is dedicated to planning and technical assistance, and $150 million of which is dedicated to capital construction. RCP shares many characteristics with the NAE program and is a part of a combined notice of funding opportunity called the Reconnecting Communities and Neighborhoods Program (U.S. Department of Transportation 2024f).

One of the major differences between the RCP and NAE programs is that the capital construction grants for the RCP require a 50% local match, compared to a 20% local match for the NAE. However, the planning grants only require a 20% local match in both the RCP and NAE (U.S. Department of Transportation 2024f).

Intermodal passenger facilities along highways and potentially other transportation facilities (e.g., railroads or transit lines) can use RCP funding to improve pedestrian, bicycle, and transit infrastructure. The RCP often gets the most attention for providing funding for freeway lids, also known as highway caps. These structures cover or cap a section of a highway, providing space for at-grade streets, green spaces, and buildings. The RCP can also fund projects that lower an interchange ramp to street level, remove an at-grade rail crossing, or realign freeway corridors into a complete street. Removing general traffic lanes and replacing them with dedicated transit lanes, protected bicycle lanes, urban greening, widened sidewalks, or improved bus stops is common with RCP projects (U.S. Department of Transportation 2024f).

FHWA Advanced Transportation Technologies and Innovation Program

The Advanced Transportation Technologies and Innovation (ATTAIN) Program, formerly known as ATTIMD, is an FHWA-administered competitive grant program dedicated to improving the safety, mobility, efficiency, system performance, intermodal connectivity, and infrastructure return on investment. ATTAIN aims to achieve these goals through the deployment, installation, and operation of advanced transportation technologies. The IIJA allocates $60 million annually to the program through 2026 (Federal Highway Administration 2023a).

ATTAIN funding can be used for the integration of transportation service payment systems—promoting cooperation between transit agencies within a metropolitan area, for example. ATTAIN funding is attractive for entities interested in developing MaaS since the IIJA introduced new eligible activities such as on-demand transportation service technologies and other shared-use mobility applications. To help drive technological advances, research and academic institutions are eligible to apply for ATTAIN funding, in addition to transit agencies, and local, regional, and state governments (Federal Highway Administration 2023a).

Funding for Airports, Ports, and Railroads

Seven programs provide funding for a variety of airport, port, and railroad projects. Table D-4 provides a general overview of the program type, matching requirements, eligible activities, funding amount through FY 2026, and typical award size of grants.

FRA

FRA Federal-State Partnership for Intercity Passenger Rail Grant Program

FRA administers the Federal-State Partnership for Intercity Passenger Rail Grant Program, which is a competitive grant program. Formerly known as the Federal-State Partnership for State of Good Repair, this program focuses on funding capital projects that reduce the state-of-good-repair backlog. The IIJA authorized a significant increase in funding to $22.5 billion through 2026, in addition to expanding the program's scope to include projects that improve performance or expand or establish new intercity passenger rail service. The IIJA authorized a significant increase in funding; $22.5 billion is allocated to the program through 2026 (Federal Railroad Administration 2024).

Table D-4.   Funding for airports, ports, and railroads.

Funding Program	Type	Local Match	Planning	Design	Construction	Stations	Transit vehicles	EV Charging	Road/Bike/Ped	Airports/Ports	FY 23–26 Funding	Typical Award Size
FRA Federal-State Partnership for Intercity Passenger Rail Grant Program	Grant	Federal share ≤ 80%	√	√	√	√					$22.5 billion	Max. award to date = $80 million
FRA Consolidated Rail Infrastructure and Safety Improvements (CRISI) Program	Grant	Minimum 20% non-federal match	√	√	√	√					$4.0 billion	Max. award to date = $58 million
FAA Airport Improvement Program (AIP)	Formula/grant	Small airports: federal share = 85%–90% Medium/large airports: federal share = 75%	√	√		√				√	$13.4 billion	Average award size = $4 million
FAA Airport Terminal Program (ATP)	Grant	Small, non-hub, primary airports: federal share = 95%; primary airports: federal share = 80%	√	√	√	√		√		√	$4.0 billion	Max. award to date = $6 million
FAA Passenger Facility Charge (PFC) Local User Fee	Fee	n/a	√	√	√	√	√	√	√	√	n/a	Max. = $4.5 fee per passenger, per flight segment
DOT Port Infrastructure Development Program (PIDP)	Grant	Federal share may not exceed 80% of total project costs (except rural/small ports)	√	√		√	√	√		√	$1.8 billion	Max. award to date = $68.7 million
FTA All Stations Accessibility Program (ASAP)	Grant	Minimum 20% non-federal match	√	√	√	√			√		$1.4 billion	Max. award to date = $254 million

Note: n/a = not applicable.

The Federal-State Partnership splits funding into two buckets: projects located within the Northeast corridor, which receive up to two-thirds of total funding, and projects located outside the Northeast corridor, which will receive at least one-third of total funding. The Federal-State Partnership features a category for station projects, which could relate to intermodal passenger facilities. Station projects can use funding to repair, replace, modernize, improve, or expand an existing station, in addition to constructing a new station (Federal Railroad Administration 2024).

FRA Consolidated Rail Infrastructure and Safety Improvements Program

The Consolidated Rail Infrastructure and Safety Improvements (CRISI) Program is an FRA grant program funding projects that improve the safety, efficiency, and reliability of intercity passenger and freight rail. The IIJA nearly tripled funding for the CRISI program, which will now award up to $1 billion in grants per year through 2026 (Federal Railroad Administration 2024).

The CRISI program dedicates at least 25% of funding to projects in rural areas. The CRISI program also sets aside at least $150 million annually for intercity passenger rail projects, $25 million for trespassing prevention, and $2 million for magnetic levitation projects. It also seeks to fund projects that address climate change, environmental justice, and racial equity (Federal Railroad Administration 2024).

Any project that enhances multimodal connections, including connections to intercity bus/rail service and commercial air service, qualifies for CRISI grants. Joint scheduling, ticketing, and baggage handling projects are among the projects that qualify for CRISI grants by facilitating service integration between rail and other modes. Additionally, capital projects that facilitate ridership growth along heavily traveled rail corridors can receive CRISI funding (Federal Railroad Administration 2024).

FAA

Airport Improvement Program

The FAA administers the Airport Improvement Program (AIP), providing grants for planning and development of public-use airports in the National Plan of Integrated Airport Systems (NPIAS). The AIP provides more than $3.35 billion annually to more than 3,300 eligible airports through entitlement funding and discretionary funding. The AIP also provides block grants to individual states for use at general aviation airports (Federal Aviation Administration 2024b).

The AIP is an important source of funding for airports across the country and provides funds for most airfield capital improvement or rehabilitation projects. Therefore, only a limited amount of AIP funding can be dedicated to intermodal passenger facilities, and this funding is limited to public-use areas (Federal Aviation Administration 2024b).

Airport Terminal Program

The Airport Terminal Program (ATP) is a new FAA discretionary program created by the IIJA that is dedicated to providing funding for terminal development projects. The goal of the program is to address the nation's aging air infrastructure. The IIJA has set aside $1 billion annually for ATP through 2026 (Federal Aviation Administration 2024a).

Large-hub airports are set to receive a maximum of 55% of total ATP funding, while medium-hub airports are allocated a maximum of 15%, small-hub airports will receive a maximum of 20%, and non-hub or non-primary airports will receive a minimum of 10% of total funding. ATP grants can be used for a variety of projects related to upgrading, rebuilding, and expanding airport terminals. The ATP was created with sustainability and multimodality in mind, which positions intermodal passenger facilities well for grants. On-airport rail access projects, for example, are specifically highlighted as an eligible activity. Projects that seek Leadership in Energy and Environmental Design (LEED) accreditation are also eligible, as well as projects to bring intermodal passenger facilities into compliance with the ADA (Federal Aviation Administration 2024a).

Passenger Facility Charge Local User Fee

Passenger facility charge (PFC) local user fees are a tool for commercial airports to fund FAA-approved enhancement projects. The FAA caps PFC fees at $4.50 per enplaned passenger, which means that an airport can charge a maximum of $18 per roundtrip for a connecting passenger (Federal Aviation Administration 2024c).

The FAA released new guidelines in 2021 regarding the eligibility of using PFC fees for on-airport rail access. Previous guidelines required that PFC fees only be utilized for on-airport rail access projects that exclusively serve airport traffic. However, this meant that rail projects where the airport station was not the terminus of the rail line were disqualified from using PFC fees. The new guidelines address this by allowing a portion of an on-airport rail access project to be funded by PFC fees. The portion of the total project costs eligible for funding from PFC fees can be based on three preferred methodologies: (1) prorated cost based on ratio of airport to ground transportation mode ridership, (2) using the cost of a hypothetical standalone spur line connecting the airport to a regional transit system, which would have met the previous guidelines, or (3) calculating the cost difference between a line that bypasses the airport and the through line (Federal Aviation Administration 2024c).

The updated guidelines from the FAA allow airports to fund better intermodal connections through PFC fees. These fees enable through-lines to the airport, which allows for more one-seat rides in both directions. Airports are expected to meet their airside needs before using PFC revenues for terminal and landside projects; if those needs are met, PFC fees are a promising revenue source for intermodal passenger facilities. All aspects of an airport station facility can be funded with PFC fees, from planning, design, and land acquisition, to construction (Federal Aviation Administration 2024c).

Maritime Administration

Port Infrastructure Development Program

The Port Infrastructure Development Program (PIDP) is a discretionary grant program for investing in port infrastructure. The Maritime Administration (MARAD) administers PIDP awards on a competitive basis. The IIJA has appropriated $450 million annually through 2026, subject to future appropriations. The PIDP will reserve 25% of funds for projects at small ports, where the statutory maximum grant award is $11.25 million (U.S. Department of Transportation Maritime Administration 2024).

While the PIDP emphasizes freight, passenger ferry terminals have also previously received funding from the program. Intermodal passenger facilities may use PIDP to rehabilitate, expand, or build a new terminal, as well as to enhance terminal access (U.S. Department of Transportation Maritime Administration 2024).

FTA

All Stations Accessibility Program

FTA's All Stations Accessibility Program (ASAP) is a competitive grant program that focuses on improving the accessibility of fixed-guideway public transportation systems. ASAP was established by the IIJA and awards $350 million annually in grants through 2026 (Federal Transit Administration 2022b).

ASAP grants can be used for the planning, design, and construction of projects at intermodal passenger facilities to meet and exceed ADA standards for buildings. ASAP grants can only be used for legacy stations or facilities that are not ADA compliant. Through repairs, modifications, and retrofits, not only can ASAP grants be used to provide access to transit systems for people with disabilities, but also can benefit bicyclists, stroller-users, passengers with luggage, and so forth to help them better utilize an intermodal passenger facility (Federal Transit Administration 2022b).

Financing Options and Innovative Delivery Strategies

Ideally, maximizing funding from the many sources described previously would cover the entire public cost of delivering a project. If there is a funding gap after all possible public funding sources have been exhausted, the remaining capital cost shortfall is generally assumed to be covered by some form of public financing or an alternative revenue source. If a funding gap is large, and available debt financing terms are less favorable or flexible, future revenue streams from the project may not be sufficient to cover the resulting debt, and the project will not be financially feasible. Maximizing funding from all possible federal, state, and local sources can minimize the funding shortfall and resulting debt issuance required (U.S. Department of Transportation 2024a).

Various financing options are available to cover the remaining costs, depending on the scenario and types of public stakeholders involved. The following describes some of the more common debt financing mechanisms available at the federal level (and state/local level, depending on the location) as well as more innovative, project-specific mechanisms that may be available for consideration for intermodal passenger facilities (U.S. Department of Transportation 2024a).

Within the context of intermodal station development potential, these additional, project-specific mechanisms generally leverage two primary opportunities that these stations tend to catalyze: (1) land use/future development potential, and (2) mobility-focused revenue-generating potential. In each case, successfully generating revenue from land use and mobility opportunities requires significant planning and time to develop and structure partnerships with the necessary public- and private-sector stakeholders. Such opportunities also have implications for the types of governance structures that may be most applicable, depending on the given scenario (U.S. Department of Transportation 2024a).

Federal Financing Mechanisms

Table D-5 summarizes the matching requirements, eligible activities, and funding amounts through FY 2026 for federal financing programs.

Table D-5. Federal financing matrix.

| Financing Program | Required Match | Eligibility | | | | | | | | Funding Amount (FY 23–26) |
		Planning	Design	Construction	Stations	Transit Vehicles	EV Charging	Road/ Bicycle/ Pedestrian	Airports/ Ports	
DOT TIFIA Credit	May not exceed 33% of the reasonably anticipated eligible project costs Up to 49% for TOD projects	√	√	√	√	√	√	√	√	$1.25 billion
DOT RRIF Credit	Direct loans for up to 100% of the project cost	√	√	√	√		√			$4.0 billion

Transportation Infrastructure Finance and Innovation Act and TIFIA 49 for Transit and TOD Projects

The Transportation Infrastructure Finance and Innovation Act (TIFIA) provides low-cost financing to fill funding gaps in infrastructure projects. TIFIA credit assistance is available in the form of direct loans, loan guarantees, and standby lines of credit to finance surface transportation projects of national and regional significance. Credit assistance has historically been capped at 33% of reasonably anticipated eligible project costs. However, in 2022, the U.S. DOT introduced the "TIFIA 49" initiative, which increases the maximum loan amount from 33% to 49% of project costs for eligible transit and TOD projects. In addition to this increase, the IIJA has made TIFIA credit assistance more attainable and flexible by (1) relaxing requirements for investment-grade ratings, and (2) increasing the maximum loan duration from 35 years to 75 years for projects with an estimated life greater than 50 years (U.S. Department of Transportation 2024a).

Recently, TIFIA loan eligibility was expanded to include port, TOD, and airport terminal and airside projects. To be eligible, these types of projects need to be added to the STIP project lists under special exceptions as TIFIA currently requires projects to be listed on the STIP (U.S. Department of Transportation 2024a).

Railroad Rehabilitation and Improvement Financing

The Railroad Rehabilitation and Improvement Financing (RRIF) program provides federal credit assistance in the form of direct loans, loan guarantees, and lines of credit to finance rail projects. RRIF offers direct loans for up to 100% of the project cost (or up to 75% for eligible TOD projects). The program allows a repayment period of up to 75 years after the date of substantial completion of the project, pursuant to the BIL. The RRIF program is authorized to provide up to $35 billion in direct loans and loan guarantees to finance development of railroad infrastructure, with $7 billion reserved for freight railroads other than Class I carriers (railroads with operating revenue of less than $272.0 million annually). Additionally, there is now a discretionary credit assistance of $50 million per year for FY 23 – FY 26, subject to appropriations, of up to $20 million per loan. At least 50% of such credit assistance is set aside for freight railroads other than Class I carriers. Furthermore, the IIJA made TOD a permanent project eligibility. Lastly, the infrastructure law codified the RRIF express program, which establishes an expedited credit review process for loans that meet certain financial and operational criteria and requires regular updates from U.S. DOT on status of application so as to reduce applicant uncertainty (U.S. Department of Transportation 2024a).

Eligible applicants for RRIF financing include railroads, state and local governments, government-sponsored authorities and corporations, limited-option freight shippers that intend to construct a new rail connection, and joint ventures that include at least one of the preceding categories. The FRA notes that RRIF financing may be used to:

- Acquire, improve, or rehabilitate intermodal or rail equipment or facilities, including track, components of track, bridges, yards, buildings and shops, and the installation of positive train control systems;
- Develop or establish new intermodal or railroad facilities;
- Reimburse planning and design expenses relating to these activities;
- Refinance outstanding debt incurred for the purposes listed previously; and
- Finance TOD (U.S. Department of Transportation 2024e).

Denver Union Station Case Study

Introduction

Appendix E, a companion to Chapter 7 and Chapter 8, and presents a case study of governance, partnerships, funding, and financing of Denver Union Station [Union Station TOD Project | RTD-Denver (https://www.rtd-denver.com/about-rtd/projects/denver-union-station)]. A transit and real estate project rolled into one, the success of Union Station derives from coordination and collaboration among numerous public and private stakeholders, combining federal funding and financing with private investment to bring the project to fruition. The project anchors the city of Denver and serves as an economic catalyst for the neighborhoods surrounding the project. RTD (Regional Transit District, Denver's regional transit agency) has estimated that the redevelopment of Union Station spurred $3.5 billion in private development in the surrounding area, with an annual economic impact of $2 billion. Private development at the station and in the surrounding area includes 3,000 residential units, 1.9 million square feet of office space, 250,000 square feet of retail uses, and 750 hotel rooms.

Evolving Governance

The development of Denver Union Station provides an excellent case study of how governance can change over time. The city of Denver originally laid out the Denver Union Station Master Plan in 2004. A supplement to the original plan was adopted in 2008 and included more concrete plans for redevelopment, including the creation of the Denver Union Station Project Authority (DUSPA), a nonprofit, public-benefit corporation formed by the City and County of Denver to finance and implement the project. Partners in DUSPA include RTD, the City and County of Denver, the Colorado Department of Transportation, and the Denver Regional Council of Governments.

Project elements were transferred to RTD, which operates and maintains them as a complete transportation district supplemented by contracts for some mobility services. Continuum and East-West Development Corporation (a joint venture called Union Station Neighborhood Corporation) is the master developer for the TOD project.

Innovative Financing

One of the challenges for the project was the Great Recession, which hit just as DUSPA was formed in 2008. Because of the resulting difficult financial market conditions, the project turned to federal financing opportunities. DUSPA, the public-benefit corporation created to finance and implement the project, secured $300 million in TIFIA and RRIF funds. It was the first time that the U.S. DOT combined a TIFIA and RRIF loan for a single project. The project was able to

Table E-1.   Denver Union Station financing.

	Transportation Infrastructure Finance and Innovation Act (TIFIA)	Railroad Rehabilitation and Improvement Financing (RRIF)
Loan amount	$146 million (30% of project cost)	$155 million (32% of project cost)
Interest rate	3.99%	3.91%
Term	31 years	29 years
Lien priority	Senior lien (rated A)	Subordinated lien (unrated)

secure these loans thanks to pledged revenue from two primary sources: the establishment of a 30-year TIF district surrounding the station, and funds from a voter-approved 0.4% sales tax increase dedicating revenues for public transit projects in Denver. Table E-1 summarizes the two financing agreements.

Federal Grants

The Denver Union Station project also benefited from various federal funding and grant programs, including FTA Section 5309 [now the Capital Investment Grants (CIG) program]. In addition, the CIG program provided $1 billion for the construction of RTD's A, B, and G Line light-rail/commuter service, which all originate at Union Station.

Public–Private Partnerships

Two master developers were involved in the project, which is also unique. Union Station Neighborhood Company focused on development of the area immediately surrounding Union Station, with the 19 acres previously owned by RTD sold off and developed by private real estate developers. The Union Station Alliance focused on the renovation of the historic station building, investing $35 million to convert it into a hotel with several ground-floor retail and restaurant tenants in the Great Hall, nicknamed "Denver's Living Room." A 99-year developer lease also includes an agreement that the hotel operator will pay for the long-term maintenance of the station building.

Value Capture

As mentioned previously, the debt service resulting from the TIFIA and RRIF loans is covered by future tax revenues from induced development. Private development at the station and in the surrounding area includes 3,000 residential units, 1.9 million square feet of office space, 250,000 square feet of retail uses, and 750 hotel rooms.